Practical Git

Confident Git Through Practice

Johan Abildskov

Apress®

Practical Git

Johan Abildskov
Tilst, Denmark

ISBN-13 (pbk): 978-1-4842-6269-6   ISBN-13 (electronic): 978-1-4842-6270-2
https://doi.org/10.1007/978-1-4842-6270-2

Managing Director, Apress Media LLC: Welmoed Spahr
Acquisitions Editor: Louise Corrigan
Development Editor: James Markham
Coordinating Editor: Nancy Chen

Cover designed by eStudioCalamar

Cover image designed by Freepik (www.freepik.com)

Distributed to the book trade worldwide by Springer Science+Business Media New York, 1 New York Plaza, New York, NY 10004. Phone 1-800-SPRINGER, fax (201) 348-4505, e-mail orders-ny@springer-sbm.com, or visit www.springeronline.com. Apress Media, LLC is a California LLC and the sole member (owner) is Springer Science + Business Media Finance Inc (SSBM Finance Inc). SSBM Finance Inc is a **Delaware** corporation.

For information on translations, please e-mail booktranslations@springernature.com; for reprint, paperback, or audio rights, please e-mail bookpermissions@springernature.com.

Apress titles may be purchased in bulk for academic, corporate, or promotional use. eBook versions and licenses are also available for most titles. For more information, reference our Print and eBook Bulk Sales web page at http://www.apress.com/bulk-sales.

Any source code or other supplementary material referenced by the author in this book is available to readers on GitHub via the book's product page, located at www.apress.com/9781484262696. For more detailed information, please visit http://www.apress.com/source-code.

Printed on acid-free paper

To my wife Anette, who managed to create the space for this book in our busy lives.

Table of Contents

About the Author

Johan Abildskov works as a DevOps Transformation Lead at Eficode in Denmark. He spends his time consulting on DevOps tooling and culture. Git has a special place in his heart. He teaches Git, talks about Git, and maintains the Git katas (`https://github.com/eficode-academy/git-katas`). He is a huge geek and a teacher at heart. He has spoken at multiple DevOpsDays and at Git Merge several times. He was on the All Things Git podcast with Ed Thomson, talking about teaching Git. He is active in meetup groups and in the DevOpsDays community, as well as speaking at both external and internal events at companies. You can find him on Twitter @RandomSort.

About the Technical Reviewer

Phil Nash is a developer evangelist for Twilio and a Google Developer Expert living in Melbourne, Australia. He loves working with Ruby or JavaScript to build web applications and tools to help developers. He once helped build a website that captured the world's favorite sandwich fillings. He has too many GitHub repositories and you can find him working on some of them live on Twitch.

Away from the keyboard, Phil listens to ska punk, enjoys discovering new beers, and runs the occasional half marathon.

Phil tweets at @philnash and you can find him elsewhere online at `https://philna.sh`.

Foreword

Even before hearing Johan present at Git Merge, I had heard about git-katas. Git-katas were introduced to me by someone in one of my classes. Immediately, I was intrigued and impressed by the hands-on, bite size exercises for learning and practicing Git. The most exciting and effective learning happens when it's in context, and with Git, that can be hard to pull off.

I've trained hundreds of developers on Git and GitHub. I can confirm that no matter what anyone tells you, using Git without understanding it is stressful, scary, and risky.

Using Git can feel like you might accidentally break everything, and not understand why. You may break it differently several times and *still* not know why. This makes learning Git alongside your daily work unappealing. Anything that you are going to do with Git, you probably are going to want to practice safely. By doing this, not only are you protecting your code and yourself, but you open up the world of curiosity. Johan's `git-katas` exercises introduce the ideal opportunity to practice and learn.

There are many nuances with using Git. I often say "there is more than one way to skin an Octocat," a turn on the idiom meaning there are many different ways to accomplish one goal. And so it is with Git: there are many different ways to accomplish a goal, and by understanding how those different ways work through building a strong mental model, you'll be able to make the right decisions and understand the implications instead of googling the right thing to type (although there's nothing wrong with that either, we all do it sometimes!).

Teaching Git presents a special challenge. It's easy to get into the details, and there are many rabbit holes in Git that one can become lost in. Johan's focus on the structure of how Git works, along with practical applications and exercises, teaches not only in a way that will ramp people up to effective daily use with Git, but in a way that fosters continuous, self-led learning that fits into the well-organized, scaffolded mental model.

Many try to teach Git the other way around; building a linear approach. Despite how the history may look, Git isn't always working as linearly as we'd like to think. By focusing on the principles and mental model, and then how the daily commands work into that model, Git can be learned in its full contexts as a distributed, snapshot-based version control tool that is meant for daily use in real world team projects.

Reading and understanding Git is one thing. Using Git in daily life is something else. But experimenting with Git, pulling it apart, making hypotheses about what to expect and then seeing what happens; that is all something entirely different. By pairing conceptual learning with hands-on activity and experimentation, Johan has built a perfect environment to not only learn about and apply Git, but to spark curiosity and a different way of thinking.

I've faced a few challenges with teaching Git. With these next questions, I'd invite you to examine where you are as you read this book, and how you can most benefit from it:

What's your experience with version control? If you haven't used version control before, then, congratulations. You are, in my opinion, in the best position to learn about Git. If you have experience with other version control systems, particularly centralized version control systems like SVN, ClearCase, TFS, etc., then you may have some unlearning to do as a part of learning Git. If you have centralized VCS experience, don't ignore the mental model of Git.

Are you comfortable with the command line? Using the command line is a requirement for this book, and is also the approach I insist upon when teaching Git. If you want to use a GUI, that's fine, but learning Git has nothing to do with using a GUI. GUIs can be great, but they also obfuscate some of the things that Git does behind the scenes. You will best be able to use Git with GUIs far more effectively and with far less uncertainty if you first practice using Git and understand it fully from the CLI.

What does "Advanced Git" mean to you? I have found that many people are scared away from Git because it's too "hard". Many other people are in search of the most "advanced" technical topics they can find, and neglect the importance of the mental model and most frequently used commands. You will learn the most from this book if you set aside expectations, both of your level of existing knowledge and of what Git topics and commands are relevant to you.

The Git community is expansive and highly technical. Even more than that, I would describe the Git community as curious and detail-oriented. Luckily, curiosity and Git pair well together. As you learn and teach Git, I encourage you to follow Johan's lead with `git-katas,` and explore your curiosity to see what happens.

Briana Swift
Senior Manager of Services Programs
Github

Acknowledgments

It is a huge privilege to be able to write a book. I owe it to my wife Anette that it has been possible, even in the midst of COVID-19, and with two tiny and awesome humans wreaking havoc.

I also owe thanks to my fantastic colleagues at Eficode, for teaching me Git, and learning together with me. In particular, I want to thank Jan Krag, Thierry Lacour, Sofus Albertsen, Christian Clausen, and Nicolaj Græsholt. I would not seem so smart about Git if it had not been for you. A second thank-you goes out to Christian Clausen for also suffering endless discussions about this book. I wish you and *Five Lines of Codes* the success you deserve.

I feel lucky to have learned so much about Git, and to have been invited into the very welcoming community around Git. I am grateful to the Git Merge community team for fantastic events and for having me on stage.

I have discovered that it is a big endeavor to write a book and that is an obvious advantage to go about it in structured and disciplined fashion. This is, to a large extent, counter to my persistent way of working. As such goes an apology to the Apress team, but most of all a thank-you for your patience and the opportunity goes out to Nancy Chen, Louise Corrigan, and James Markham. A special thank-you goes to Phil Nash whose constructive feedback raised not just the technical level of the book but also helped shape the learning path.

Introduction

Git is a tool that software developers use every day, yet many developers do not feel confident with the basic operations of Git and lose their cool when they leave the happy path. Git is so pervasive that it is unlikely that you will work in a setting where you are not using Git to develop your software. This means that you will get tremendous return on investment on your efforts to build your Git skills. You will be a better, more productive software engineer, every day, because you have learned Git thoroughly.

The book before you takes a hands-on approach to learning, and should you choose to skimp on the exercises, you will be missing out on a big part of the learning. One thing is the awareness I can give you through the written word, but it will not fasten itself and become an active tool in your mind until you have applied it.

The exercises that we are using in this book are designed to be repeatable. Just like a martial artist will go through the forms of movements until they are flowing freely and become muscle memory, so can you go through the Git katas presented in this book until you become proficient.

First, we build the right mental models, so we are sure we are thinking the right way around Git concepts. I recommend you do not skip this, even if you have been using Git already.

When we have covered the mental models, we dive into the basic Git functionality, creating the snapshots or versions of our working directory that we can later jump between with ease. We lay these snapshots out in a usable history in Chapters 3 and 4.

In Chapter 5, we go through common models of collaboration on source code using Git.

With these foundations in place, we end on three advanced chapters on manipulating Git history, customizing Git, and finally some Git internals.

I hope you enjoy the book, the exercises, and will feel more confident in your further work with Git.

CHAPTER 1

Git Intuition

We've all tried it. We get our Git repository in some inconsistent and irreconcilable state. We have found many solutions on Stack Overflow and hesitantly pasted into our command lines. But after each attempt at getting back to a sane state, we feel ourselves sliding further and further away from resolving our Git problem. So we delete our local repository, clone the repository, and start over. I know I have been in that situation more than once. This situation is widespread and is symptomatic of a lack of intuition about how Git works. We tend to choose the path of least resistance, and in Git terms, that means we learn to commit, push, and pull. In some cases, we learn to work with branches, but we become uncomfortable if we veer away from the happy path. This book wants to avoid precisely that. We will build a solid foundation of intuition on top of which we'll apply concrete commands and solutions. This allows us to first reason about the situations we find ourselves in and then select the right solution from our toolkit. Because we have practiced, we can apply the solution with confidence.

This book wants to avoid precisely that. We will build a solid foundation of intuition on top of which we'll apply concrete commands and solutions. This allows us to first reason about the situations we find ourselves in and then select the right solution from our toolkit. Because we have practiced, we can apply the solution with confidence.

This chapter will build our intuition at a high level, and we will do our first investigations of how that intuition maps to Git commands and how our workspace and repository reflect these commands.

Version Control

In this section, we will cover what types of issues and what concrete problems we try to solve when we are using Git. This is the foundation and motivation for our entire endeavor. Git is a version control system, but what does that mean in our day-to-day life?

Git is also known as a content-addressable file system. This is something that permeates the entire way Git perceives the world and sets the boundary for what can

© Johan Abildskov 2020
J. Abildskov, *Practical Git*, https://doi.org/10.1007/978-1-4842-6270-2_1

be done with Git. What this implies though is that Git, at its core, is about managing files. When interacting with Git, we either manage versions of files and directories or investigate the history of a workspace.

Many of us have ended up in a situation like Figure 1-1, where we have a workspace with different versions of a project copied around, based on some arbitrary naming convention. This is how it ends up when we do not actively version control our software.

ProjectX	⋮
ProjectX_Draft	⋮
ProjectX_Final	⋮
ProjectX_Final _FINAL	⋮
ProjectX_Latest	⋮
ProjectX_Latest - Kopi	⋮

Figure 1-1. *Folders in a workspace with ambiguous naming, making it nonobvious what the newest version is and how they relate*

This ad hoc approach causes all sorts of difficult challenges. An important point to make here is that none of these issues or challenges are inherent in the problems that we are trying to solve or in the way we work. The tools are freely available; it is simply a choice to work in an improper way. The following is a list of things that are impossible or unnecessarily hard when working directly in the file system:

- How does each folder relate to each other?

- What is the latest version?

- What is the difference between two specific versions?

- What is the common base for two product variants?

- How do I revert a specific change in a product variant?

- At what point in time was this change introduced, and by whom?

- How do I merge these two folders?

In Figure 1-2, I show how the same folders could be united in a graph of workspaces. This allows us to maintain a sense of how our software evolves over time.

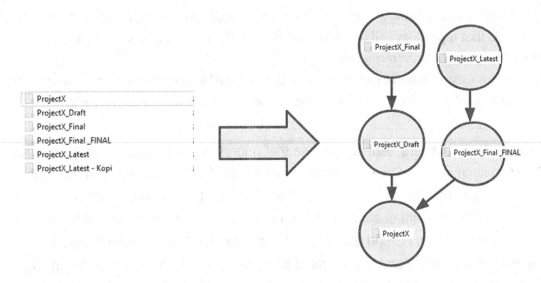

Figure 1-2. *The folders from Figure 1-1 maps over in a graph of workspaces. This increases our understanding of the history tremendously*

These problems and much more are what Git solves for developers worldwide every day. Before we go in and investigate our first Git repository, we need some of the basic concepts described. Language is a powerful way to convey understanding, so I recommend you try to be as pedantic as possible when talking about Git. This will help you internalize the concepts. When you are a master, you can be as vague as you want.

Basic Git Concepts

Now that I have provided a very rudimentary overview of the type of problems, I will dive into the basic building blocks that we need to build an understanding of Git.

The Repository

When we talk about Git at the high level, we talk about collaborating in repositories. Many software developers share their code as open source on platforms like GitHub or GitLab. Each software project is represented by one or more repositories, depending on what strategy the organization behind the project contains. In many cases, a repository represents a single source component, such as a software library or a product you can download and run on your computer or website.

For most of this book, we will be working in a single repository, and for most of the book, that repository will be local. That is, we will not collaborate or use an online platform to synchronize our repository to.

A repository contains all the information that is available about our versioned workspace. This includes all the commits, all the references, and the entire history of the repository.

Note   New Git users, especially those that migrate in from another version control system such as ClearCase or SVN, worry about the fact that the entire repository resides locally on the developer's PC. They fear that the repository will take an unreasonable amount of space and that operations will be slow. Going into detail on this topic is way beyond the scope of this book. The short answer is that it is unlikely to become a problem for most workflows, and if it becomes a bottleneck, there are tools and strategies to handle this.

All Git commands run in the context of a repository. This is true no matter if we are running simple commands to interact with our local repository or doing more complex collaborative online commands. All the exercises used in this book run in the context of a repository, and all the work you will do in your day-to-day life does as well. There are two common ways of starting work in a repository. We can either use the command `git init` to initialize a new local repository without any history and start our work there. This can even be done in a folder with content that is not under version control yet. More commonly, we use the command git clone to obtain a copy of a repository. The source of a repository is most often a private (i.e., Bitbucket on premises) or public (i.e., GitHub cloud) repository manager. If we are using the `clone` command, we often call it *cloning* a repository, and we call the local instance of the repository a *clone*.

The local repository is tied to the source by a configuration called the *remote*. Unless you are working with open source software, you are unlikely to work with more than a single remote. Open source software is often developed with a so-called "fork-based" workflow that we will cover in a later chapter. Collaboration is generally done by pushing and pulling changes between local and remote repositories. How that is done will be covered later.

In short, a repository is the totality of the history of a software project. That is all committed together with metadata. A repository allows you to work with version control locally and collaborate with others through remote repositories.

Note   Some commercial software development works internally using fork-based workflows. This can happen because of different trust levels or low maturity in the software engineering department. It is my opinion that fork-based workflows are an antipattern, or at best a workaround in that situation. Google-based research showed that a key factor in perceived developer productivity is the visibility and availability of source code also from outside the team.

The Commit

The base unit of Git is the commit. Intuitively, a Git commit represents the full state of the workspace at a given point in time. A commit also contains the following metadata:

- What commit(s) came before it
- The author and committer
- A timestamp
- A commit message, with information on the content of the commit

Caution   New commits are never created without reason. Their creation is initiated by the user. This can give cause to some frustration for new users, who do not understand why they do not see their changes in shared repositories. What often happens is that the user tries to share all their new code, but without having created a new commit, the shared repository is already up to date without the newest changes. Make sure you commit, before sharing.

The previous commit is called the parent. We can see that we create a graph of commits, tied together through the parent pointers in commits. Commits can have zero, one, or many parents.

The most common scenario is commits with one parent. This happens when we are moving along a single strain or chain – creating one version after another.

The very first commit in a repository is special as it has zero parents. This makes sense as nothing comes before the first commit. The first commit is also often referred to as the initial commit. Many repositories' first commit has the message "Initial Commit" indicating it as the start of the versioned history. If we see large first commits, this is often a sign that the developers did too much work before considering version control. This is bad as version control should never be an afterthought. But you are here, so you will of course never again end up in this situation.

A commit can also have an arbitrarily large number of parents. A commit ends up with more than one parent when branches are merged. We will cover that later, so don't worry about that now. I say that commits can have an arbitrarily large number of parents, and this is true. The Linux kernel is a fun place to go to see Git used to its limits. Linus Torvalds, the inventor of Linux and Git, has a notorious fondness for the octopus merge where many branches are merged in one fell swoop. This workflow obviously works for the Linux kernel and other open source projects, but my recommendation is that if you end up in a situation where you are merging more than two branches, you are likely doing it wrong.

In short, a Git commit is a bundle representing a workspace that we can retrieve and investigate at any point in time, at lightning speed.

The Branch and the Tag

Git has two types of things, objects and references. The commits that we have described earlier are immutable and in the category called objects. The other category of useful things is called references and is much more lightweight.

At this point, I will introduce two types of references, branches and tags. Both point at specific commits in the graph that we build using commits as described earlier.

The Tag

The tag is the simplest reference in Git. It is simply a pointer to a commit. A commit use for tags is marking the commits that were released with a tag named after the concrete version.

In Figure 1-3, we see a commit with a tag; this allows us to reference to this commit without using its sha.

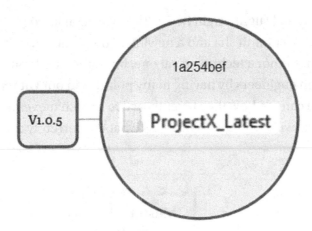

Figure 1-3. A tag is pointing to commit <SHA>

A tag is never changing. That means that we at any time can back to a commit through a name. It is much easier to understand what is going on when discussing what happened in "V1.0" rather than a long sha.

The Branch

In my experience, branches both give cause to great power and much frustration for developers. There is no reason for this frustration though. It is often the mental model that is lacking from simply using Git without proper education. Visualizing the Git graph and branches is a power move that is available to all.

A branch is like a tag except that a branch is supposed to move. As we do development and create commits, the currently active branch moves along and points to the new commits that we create. The currently active branch is also said to be the branch that we have checked out.

Note   While it is not strictly necessary to have a branch checked out, it is considered best practice to do so, and I'd argue that in all cases during normal development, you are going to have a branch checked out. When you have checked something other than a branch out, you will end up in the so-called detached head state, which sounds more dangerous than it is. We will later cover both how to end up in this state and how to safely recover.

Branches are extremely lightweight in Git. They weigh in at no more than 41 bytes. These bytes represent a commit sha and a newline. This means that the primary cost of having many branches is not a technological one, but rather it is limited by the cognitive overhead imposed on engineers by having many pointers in our Git repository.

In Figure 1-4, we can see how the currently active branch moves along as we create multiple commits. We will cover how Git knows what the currently active branch is, in Chapter 4.

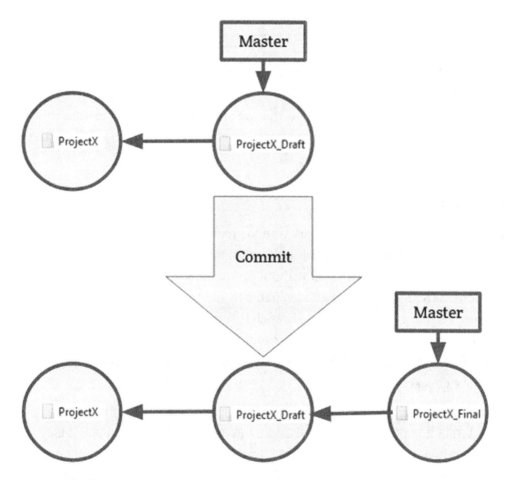

Figure 1-4. *A Git branch moves as more commits are created*

Git uses a branch named master as its default. This means that we expect the master branch to be the main source of truth and the most important branch. In other version control systems, this could be called Trunk or Mainline. There are a few conventions that expect the default branch to be named master, and I highly recommend that you do not name your single source of truth branch to something other than master. Do so at your own peril. It is highly unlikely to solve any real problems.

In Git, we can have many branches, but it is recommended that we have a low amount of long-lived or permanent branches. In my experience, the need for anything more than one permanent branch is artificial and construed. Having many branches often causes too complex workflows to arise, generating overhead in the development process. Complex workflows are often introduced to create higher-quality, safer integrations, and other things of that ilk, but often, they are at best treating symptoms of deeper problems with the way of working in the software.

Setting Up Git and the Git Katas

Now that we have introduced the foundational vocabulary, we are going to make sure that everything is set up. Then, we can dive in and get our hands dirty on actual Git repositories and do some deliberate practice there. I tend to put everything in Git repositories, so you will not be surprised to learn that the exercises that we are going to be using in this book are delivered to you as a Git repository.

That is why we will be introducing our first command now. As mentioned before, Git is a distributed version control system. In your day-to-day life, you are very likely to collaborate on a repository that is hosted in the cloud or on premise on one of the many repository managers. We use the Git clone command to obtain a local copy of the repository to do our work in.

Git Clone

A clone is a two-step command: first, it downloads the Git repository, and then, it checks out the most recent commit on the default branch of the repository into the workspace.

First off, this enables you to change files, compile code, and run tests – all the tasks that you commonly perform in a workspace with source code. Secondly, as you download the entire repository during the clone, you can compare different revisions of the code and do all possible version control commands, at local speed in your repository.

There are many variants of the clone command, but in its basic form, it looks like this: `git clone <remote-repository> <local-path>`. An example of this is `git clone https://github.com/eficode-academy/git-katas.git git-katas`. This will download the repository containing the git katas into the folder `git-katas/.git/` and check out the workspace of the newest commit on the `master` branch into the folder `git-katas`.

The .git Folder

One of my goals with this book is to take the magic out of Git and turn it into an awesome tool that you can wield. A part of Git than many find vexing is the .git folder. But while it feels like a magical folder that shows up in your workspace, it is rather a source of sanity in what can be an abstract world.

We will not dive into details on the many things that are in the .git folder, but for the purpose of intuition, let it suffice that it, among other things, contains

- The entire history of the repository, including data

- Local configuration

- Pointer to what is currently checked out

- Pointer to the origin that was cloned from

This is by no means a complete list, but it underlines one very important point: when you clone a repository, you get the entire repository on your local computer. There are ways to get a smaller subset of a repository, but assume that you get the full repository and that it will not be a cause of performance issues or unnecessary space usage. Rather it allows you to work offline, asynchronous, and at the speed of your local system.

With the clone command nicely introduced, we will go into the first exercise and download the exercises that we will be using.

SETTING UP GIT AND THE KATAS

The time has come for the command line to come in place. I will be showing all commands executed through Git Bash in Windows. This command-line environment is shipped with the Git installed with Windows and is compatible with common shells on Linux and Mac, so everything should be recognizable to you, no matter your platform of choice. Some users report issues if using the zsh command line. If you experience this, please run the exercises in bash.

Checking Git is working

First up, we are going to open a command line and run the git --version command to check everything is working as expected.

- Open your favorite command prompt.

- Execute at any location the command git --version.

- You should see the version of Git that you are running being output in the command line.

The expected outcome should be as the following snippet:

```
$ git --version
git version 2.25.0.windows.1
```

What we get is the installed version of Git. In my case, it is version 2.25.0.windows.1. This is the newest version of Git at the time of writing. I recommend you update to this version. There are many good things both performance and UX wise being released in Git. So keep up with the versions.

Retrieving the Git katas

The exercises that we are going to use to practice the concepts we are introducing is called the Git katas and can be obtained through GitHub.

This exercise will take you through the process of cloning the Git katas repository and checking that you have the entire set of exercises present, before we dive into concrete exercises using Git. If you do not feel comfortable with basic shell commands, now would be an opportune moment to read on on those.

1. Start a command line: Open a terminal of your liking and prepare to execute commands in it.

2. Navigate to the location where you prefer to store your source code. I prefer to store my files in ~/repos/organization/repo.

3. Clone the Git katas using the clone command:

    ```
    git clone https://github.com/eficode-academy/git-katas.git
    git-katas
    ```

4. cd to the git-katas folder and use ls to see the list of exercises.

If I run through the aforementioned commands, it looks like as follows:

```
$ cd ~/repos/randomsort

$ git clone https://github.com/eficode-academy/git-katas.git git-katas
Cloning into 'git-katas'...
remote: Enumerating objects: 34, done.
remote: Counting objects: 100% (34/34), done.
remote: Compressing objects: 100% (31/31), done.
remote: Total 1690 (delta 16), reused 7 (delta 3), pack-reused 1656
Receiving objects: 100% (1690/1690), 486.60 KiB | 1.72 MiB/s, done.
Resolving deltas: 100% (708/708), done.

$ cd git-katas

$ ls
3-way-merge/                    basic-staging/               ff-merge/
merge-driver/       rebase-interactive-autosquash/  test.ps1
advanced-rebase-interactive/  basic-stashing/                git-attributes/
merge-mergesort/  reorder-the-history/           test.sh
amend/                          bisect/                      git-tag/
objects/            reset/                           utils/
bad-commit/                     commit-on-wrong-branch/
ignore/             Overview.md         reverted-merge/
basic-branching/                commit-on-wrong-branch-2/
images/             pre-push/           save-my-commit/
basic-cleaning/                 configure-git/
investigation/      README.md           SHELL-BASICS.md
basic-commits/                  detached-head/               LICENSE.txt
rebase-branch/      squashing/
basic-revert/                   docs/                        merge-conflict/
rebase-exec/        submodules/

$
```

There is a lot going on in this tiny example. First off, we get a lot of output from the clone command, but luckily, we can ignore it, unless we are trying to debug something. Secondly, there are two things that we can leave out and that most people commonly ignore. We can often ignore the .git part of the remote repository and have Git and the repository manager sort that out. Many people ignore the last part of the command. This will clone the repository into a folder that has the name of the repository, here shown by example:

```
$ git clone https://github.com/eficode-academy/git-katas
Cloning into 'git-katas'...
remote: Enumerating objects: 34, done.
remote: Counting objects: 100% (34/34), done.
remote: Compressing objects: 100% (31/31), done.
remote: Total 1690 (delta 16), reused 7 (delta 3), pack-reused 1656
Receiving objects: 100% (1690/1690), 486.60 KiB | 1.72 MiB/s, done.
Resolving deltas: 100% (708/708), done.

$ ls git-katas
3-way-merge/                basic-staging/              ff-merge/
merge-driver/       rebase-interactive-autosquash/  test.ps1
advanced-rebase-interactive/  basic-stashing/          git-attributes/
merge-mergesort/   reorder-the-history/               test.sh
amend/                      bisect/                     git-tag/
objects/            reset/                          utils/
bad-commit/                 commit-on-wrong-branch/
ignore/             Overview.md      reverted-merge/
basic-branching/            commit-on-wrong-branch-2/
images/             pre-push/        save-my-commit/
basic-cleaning/             configure-git/
investigation/      README.md        SHELL-BASICS.md
basic-commits/              detached-head/              LICENSE.txt
rebase-branch/      squashing/
basic-revert/               docs/                       merge-conflict/
rebase-exec/        submodules/
```

As you can see in the preceding data in most cases, this is enough to obtain the desired outcome. That reduces the command we need to remember to git clone <repository>.

Troubleshooting: If you are typing the clone command and get a "permission denied" error, it might be because you have misspelled the URL. Try copy pasting the command, and see if it works.

Now that you have been through the first of our exercises, you have made sure that you have Git installed and working, and you also have the Git katas downloaded so we can use them for the rest of the book.

Getting Our Bearings in a Repository

Now, we come to the important part: working in a Git repository.

In this part, we will be using a few Git commands to look around inside of a repository and a few shell commands to navigate the workspace as we interact with Git.

We will be introducing the commands: status, log, and checkout.

We will cover status in depth, but log and checkout are both big commands that we will introduce gradually over the course of the book.

Git Status

When I teach Git, I always tell my students: "If you are in doubt of what is going or, or what you are supposed to do, just run `git status` and Git will tell you." While this is a slight exaggeration, all inquiries should start with a `git status`.

Git status tells you about the state of your workspace and how it compares to what is currently checked out. If the workspace is identical to what is checked out, the workspace is said to be clean. If the workspace contains changes, of any sort, the workspace is said to be dirty. Changes can be modified, deleted, added, or renamed files. Git also has a notion of ignored paths, and from the perspective of Git, changes in ignored paths do not make the workspace dirty. How a file moves through these states is shown in Figure 1-5.

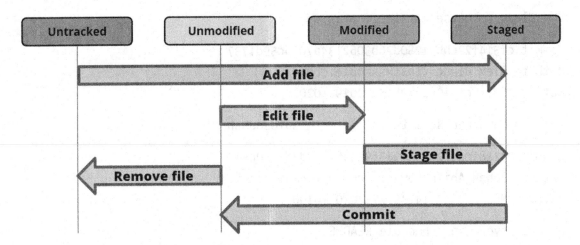

Figure 1-5. *The different states a file can be in and the actions that transition between them*

Git Log

As we are in the universe of version control, being able to look at what versions exist and how they relate to each other is an essential feature. Git log is the most basic way we can look at the history of our repository. While Git log is a basic command, it is also one of the most configurable ones, and the number of flags and arguments can be intimidating. Do not despair, I will guide you to use log confidently.

If you look in the following listing, you see a run of log without any commands and flags, configured with the default Git 2.25 installation. In this repository, there are only a few commits, on a single branch, and a single tag. Commits come in reverse chronological order, meaning that the newest commit will be the one printed first and then following the parent pointer of each commit until we reach the first commit.

Each commit contains a lot of information in this view. All the data here is printed per commits, and this behavior is often too verbose for most uses. We can also see the references and the commits they point to.

```
$ git log
commit 335e019ac148297bd938f137ea9c7cf617c07576 (HEAD -> master, origin/
master, origin/HEAD)
Author: Johan Sigfred Abildskov <randomsort@gmail.com>
Date:   Thu Feb 13 11:10:55 2020 +0100
```

```
    Clean up unused trainer-notes.md

commit c1514f22ebb31280d26b3062134a7066c59df737
Author: Alex Blanc <test@example.com>
Date:    Sat Oct 19 17:38:32 2019 +0200

    Add kata Rebase Interactive with autosquash

commit 032a8fcdef22a53f123f914a8b7b2d7d87cdd2e7
Author: Johan Abildskov <randomsort@gmail.com>
Date:    Mon Feb 10 14:35:27 2020 +0100

    Fix typos in submodule README
```

As mentioned earlier, the verbosity of the log command is not very useful
for getting an overview, so over the next few listings, we will configure our log command
to become more succinct. First, we will use the flag --oneline to the same log command
as earlier, to get a more condensed view of the log. The entire command becomes
git log --oneline, and the resulting output can be seen in the following listing (next
listing!). The oneline flag truncates the commit message to only the subject and the sha
to a shorter prefix. This makes it a lot easier to get an overview.

```
$ git log --oneline
335e019 (HEAD -> master, origin/master, origin/HEAD) Clean up unused
trainer-notes.md
c1514f2 Add kata Rebase Interactive with autosquash
032a8fc Fix typos in submodule README
262c478 Fix three typos
1e07423 Expand  on  submodules kata
1ef8902 Use explicit numbering
dbfccc8 Added pointer to Overview also as Learning Path
1848caf Reordered katas on Overview and added missing ones
```

If we are missing the references from the preceding view, it can be due to an
outdated version of Git. In that case, we can use the flag --decorate to have Git
annotate the commits with the relevant pointers. Our command then becomes
git log --oneline --decorate. In newer versions of Git, decorate is the
default --oneline behavior. An example of how it would look like with an older
version of Git can be simulated using the flag --no-decoration.

```
$ git log --oneline
335e019  Clean up unused trainer-notes.md
c1514f2 Add kata Rebase Interactive with autosquash
032a8fc Fix typos in submodule README
262c478 Fix three typos
1e07423 Expand  on  submodules kata
1ef8902 Use explicit numbering
dbfccc8 Added pointer to Overview also as Learning Path
1848caf Reordered katas on Overview and added missing ones
```

As long as we are only using one branch and thus have a linear history with no divergent threads of development, this should be enough for our use. When we look into more complex histories in Chapter 3, we will add some more tools to our log command. There is however one flag that is tremendously useful for restricting the number of commits that we get in the log output. We can use the flag -n <number> to limit the number of entries in the log output to <number>. For small numbers, we can use the literal number as the flag. For example, git log -3 will only output three commits. In Listing 6 we run with the flags --oneline, --decorate, and -n 2.

```
335e019 (HEAD -> master, origin/master, origin/HEAD) Clean up unused
trainer-notes.md
c1514f2 Add kata Rebase Interactive with autosquash
```

Note   You can use gitk instead of git log to get a prettier GUI-based output. Some prefer this, and few know they can get this nice overview without using a full-fledged GUI Git client like Sourcetree or Git kraken. You can use gitk without arguments like so: gitk.

Summary

In this chapter, we introduced the basic problem space that we are working with, namely, maintaining and relating multiple versions of a collection of files and directories. We also made sure that Git was installed and downloaded the Git katas using the command git clone. Then, we briefly looked at the history of a tiny repository using git log.

CHAPTER 2

Building Commits

In this chapter, we will cover commits in detail. Commits are the basic building blocks of our history, both containing the actual content of our versions and the parent pointers that define our history. Deliberately fashioning commits and attaching well-formed commit messages to them are foundational skills needed to be a valuable individual contributor in a collaborative setting.

What's in a Workspace

At its core, Git is about files and directories. In software development, the place where we store project-specific files with our code is commonly called the workspace. When I refer to our workspace, I refer to the root folder of our project, containing the files and directories that constitute the project, and also the .git folder. In the following snippet, we see a directory listing both in shell and in Windows Explorer. Notice how the .git folder containing the Git repository is hidden. It is a common convention to have files and folders that start with a `.` be hidden.

```
$ ls
images/  index.js  library.js  README.md
```

As mentioned, our workspace can be either dirty or clean, when compared to the currently checked-out commit on the repository. Dirty is not a bad word; it simply implies different. This difference is of course a good thing because those are the changes that we have made, but just have not committed yet. Another source that can make our workspace dirty is autogenerated files and build artifacts. We will later cover how we can make Git ignore certain paths.

We can look at our workspace as always being represented by a commit and a changeset or diff applied on top of that. Figure 2-1 shows how the objects are identical in a clean workspace and the repository.

© Johan Abildskov 2020
J. Abildskov, *Practical Git*, https://doi.org/10.1007/978-1-4842-6270-2_2

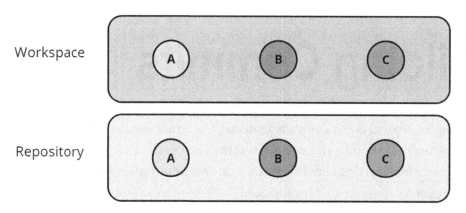

Figure 2-1. *A clean workspace on top of a repository*

As the contents of the workspace and the repository are identical, the workspace is considered clean. In Figure 2-2, we can see how a dirty workspace relates to the repository when we change the file A.

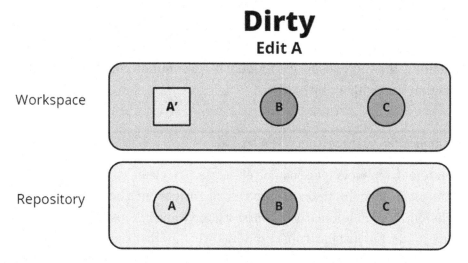

Figure 2-2. *A dirty workspace after changing file A on top of the repository*

We can see this using the Git status command. As we change files in the repository and run the git status command, we can see how Git tells us that files become modified or deleted for files that are already tracked by Git, or how files that we add to our workspace for the first time show up in Git status as untracked.

```
$ ls
A  B  C  D
$ git status
On branch master
nothing to commit, working tree clean
$ echo testing > A
$ git status
On branch master
nothing to commit, working tree clean
$ git add A
$ git status
On branch master
nothing to commit, working tree clean
$ git commit -m 'Edit A'
On branch master
nothing to commit, working tree clean
$ git status
On branch master
nothing to commit, working tree clean
$ rm B
$ git status
On branch master
Changes not staged for commit:
  (use "git add/rm <file>..." to update what will be committed)
  (use "git checkout -- <file>..." to discard changes in working directory)

        deleted:    B

no changes added to commit (use "git add" and/or "git commit -a")
$ git commit -am 'Remove B'
[master db1f9c6] Remove B
 1 file changed, 0 insertions(+), 0 deletions(-)
```

```
 delete mode 100644 B
$ git status
On branch master
nothing to commit, working tree clean
$ touch D
$ git status
On branch master
nothing to commit, working tree clean
$ git add D
$ git status
On branch master
nothing to commit, working tree clean
$ git commit -m 'Add D'
On branch master
nothing to commit, working tree clean
$ git status
On branch master
nothing to commit, working tree clean
```

Preparing Commits Using the Stage

In Git, files can be represented in three different locations, of which we have covered two so far: the workspace and the repository. There is a third one that lies between the two – that area is called the index or the stage. The logic of this stage is that it is the place where we fashion what will go into the commit that we make next. The flow of work goes as follows: We make some changes, we stage the changes that we want to be a part of the next commit, and finally we make a commit. Rinse and repeat. This flow can be seen in Figure 2-3.

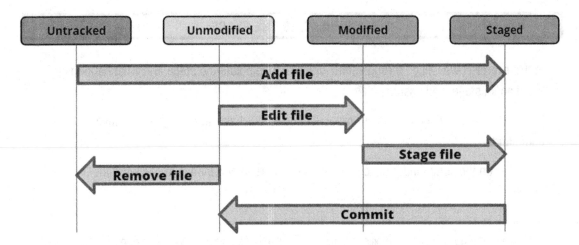

Figure 2-3. *Flow inside a local repository*

This flow is a simplified view of normal software development flow, but hopefully, it is recognizable. The best intuitive description of the stage I've ever heard is that we imagine we are the photographer at a family reunion, and we are instructing people on who should go on the next picture, and when we are done with that, we take the photograph. Then, we repeat. In a similar fashion, we use the command add to add a path to the stage. This action is also called staging a file.

Note   When we stage a file or directory, we do not stage simply a path that we tell Git to include in the next commit. We stage the content at the point when we run the `git add` command. This means that if we change a file after staging it, we need to stage it again, to include it in the next commit.

As we saw in Figure 2-3, a file can be in a few different states from the perspective of Git. The following list omits only a final state that we will cover later in this chapter:

- **Unmodified**: This file is identical in the workspace and in currently checked-out commit in the repository.

- **Modified**: This file is present in both workspace and repository, but is different.

- **Staged**: This file is in the workspace, current commit, and stage. Note that the file can be different in all three locations.

- **Untracked**: This file is in the workspace, but not in the current commit.

MANIPULATING THE STAGE

In this exercise, we will go through some steps to manipulate the stage and what happens as we change, stage, and unstage files.

First, let's see how things are in our repository using our basic toolkit of investigative commands.

First, we run the command pwd to see the path we are in and then ls to see what the directory contains.

```
$ pwd
/c/Users/rando/repos/randomsort/practical-git/chapter2/stage-repo
$ ls
file1.txt   subfolder/
$ ls -al
total 9
drwxr-xr-x 1 rando 197609  0 mar 13 12:18 ./
drwxr-xr-x 1 rando 197609  0 mar 13 12:18 ../
drwxr-xr-x 1 rando 197609  0 mar 13 12:19 .git/
-rw-r--r-- 1 rando 197609 14 mar 13 12:18 file1.txt
drwxr-xr-x 1 rando 197609  0 mar 13 12:18 subfolder/
```

Notice how the .git folder does not show until we use the flag -a. This is because `ls` by default does not show hidden folders, and as mentioned, the convention is that files and folders starting with a period (.) are considered hidden. Other than that, we can see that we have a few files and a single directory.

Now that we have gotten the basic outlook on the file system, we use a few basic git commands to get a hold on the repository. We use git status to ask Git about the state of our workspace compared to our repository. We get more information that we will ignore until a later chapter.

```
$ git status
On branch master
nothing to commit, working tree clean
$ git log --oneline --decorate
1cc4f2e (HEAD -> master) Initial commit
```

What we get from git status is first off the confirmation that we are indeed working inside a Git repository. We also learn that our workspace is clean and nothing is staged. From git log, we learn that we have a repository with a very brief history.

In the following steps, we will make changes to the workspace and stage files along the way. We will continuously use Git status to see how our actions are reflected in the states of the files. Remember we start with a clean workspace.

```
$ echo "test" > file1.txt

$ git status
On branch master
Changes not staged for commit:
  (use "git add <file>..." to update what will be committed)
  (use "git restore <file>..." to discard changes in working directory)
        modified:   file1.txt

no changes added to commit (use "git add" and/or "git commit -a")

$ git add file1.txt

$ git status
On branch master
Changes to be committed:
  (use "git restore --staged <file>..." to unstage)
        modified:   file1.txt

$ echo thing > file1.txt

$ git status
On branch master
Changes to be committed:
  (use "git restore --staged <file>..." to unstage)
        modified:   file1.txt

Changes not staged for commit:
  (use "git add <file>..." to update what will be committed)
  (use "git restore <file>..." to discard changes in working directory)
        modified:   file1.txt

$ echo content > file_that_did_not_exist_before.txt
```

```
$ git status
On branch master
Changes to be committed:
  (use "git restore --staged <file>..." to unstage)
        modified:   file1.txt

Changes not staged for commit:
  (use "git add <file>..." to update what will be committed)
  (use "git restore <file>..." to discard changes in working directory)
        modified:   file1.txt

Untracked files:
  (use "git add <file>..." to include in what will be committed)
        file_that_did_not_exist_before.txt

$ git add file
file_that_did_not_exist_before.txt   file1.txt

$ git add file
file_that_did_not_exist_before.txt   file1.txt

$ git add file_that_did_not_exist_before.txt

$ git status
On branch master
Changes to be committed:
  (use "git restore --staged <file>..." to unstage)
        modified:   file1.txt
        new file:   file_that_did_not_exist_before.txt

Changes not staged for commit:
  (use "git add <file>..." to update what will be committed)
  (use "git restore <file>..." to discard changes in working directory)
        modified:   file1.txt

$ echo content > subfolder/subfile1.txt

$ echo content > subfolder/subfile2.txt
```

```
$ git status
On branch master
Changes to be committed:
  (use "git restore --staged <file>..." to unstage)
        modified:   file1.txt
        new file:   file_that_did_not_exist_before.txt

Changes not staged for commit:
  (use "git add <file>..." to update what will be committed)
  (use "git restore <file>..." to discard changes in working directory)
        modified:   file1.txt

Untracked files:
  (use "git add <file>..." to include in what will be committed)
        subfolder/subfile1.txt
        subfolder/subfile2.txt

$ git add subfolder/
$ git status
On branch master
Changes to be committed:
  (use "git restore --staged <file>..." to unstage)
        modified:   file1.txt
        new file:   file_that_did_not_exist_before.txt
        new file:   subfolder/subfile1.txt
        new file:   subfolder/subfile2.txt

Changes not staged for commit:
  (use "git add <file>..." to update what will be committed)
  (use "git restore <file>..." to discard changes in working directory)
        modified:   file1.txt

$ git restore --staged file1.txt

$ git status
On branch master
Changes to be committed:
```

```
        (use "git restore --staged <file>..." to unstage)
        new file:   file_that_did_not_exist_before.txt
        new file:   subfolder/subfile1.txt
        new file:   subfolder/subfile2.txt

Changes not staged for commit:
  (use "git add <file>..." to update what will be committed)
  (use "git restore <file>..." to discard changes in working directory)
        modified:   file1.txt

$ git commit -m "our first commit"
[master de09faa] our first commit
 3 files changed, 3 insertions(+)
 create mode 100644 file_that_did_not_exist_before.txt
 create mode 100644 subfolder/subfile1.txt
 create mode 100644 subfolder/subfile2.txt

$ git status
On branch master
Changes not staged for commit:
  (use "git add <file>..." to update what will be committed)
  (use "git restore <file>..." to discard changes in working directory)
        modified:   file1.txt

no changes added to commit (use "git add" and/or "git commit -a")

$ git log --oneline --decorate
de09faa (HEAD -> master) our first commit
1cc4f2e Initial commit
```

In the preceding list, we see a few noteworthy items.

- When we change the file1.txt after we have staged it, it becomes both modified and staged.

- We can have both modified and added files in the same stage.

- When we stage a directory, all subpaths are staged.

- We can undo the staging of a path using git restore --staged <path>.

Committing

In the previous section, we spent a lot of energy discussing how we could control what would be part of our commits. In this section, we will cover how we do the actual persisting where we persist the content of the stage into the repository in the bundle we call a commit.

Git Commit

To create commits, we use the command `git commit`. Figure 2-4 shows the different steps of the commit flow. It assumes we have added some changes to the stage. What then happens is the message passed with the command-line flag `-m` and the changeset and some automatically generated content is persisted in the commit object. Afterward, the currently checked-out branch is updated to point to this newly created commit.

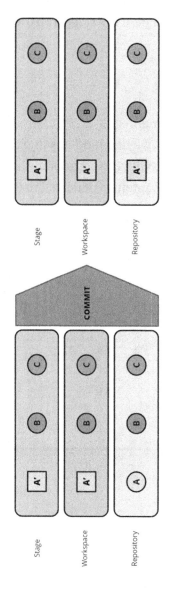

Figure 2-4. *This is what happens when we run the command* git commit *assuming files are staged*

As mentioned before, we actively control two parts of the commit, while the rest is handled automatically by Git. We defined what the file content will be of the commit using the stage, while we control what message will be attached to the commit when we create the commit.

The most common way of specifying the commit message is using the flag -m and passing the commit message directly in the command. This method has the advantage that the commit message is likely to be short and concise, and we do not have an extra step in the process of creating a commit. There are several disadvantages to this; we will cover these a bit later when we discuss what constitutes a good commit message. The most basic commit flow looks like as follows in the command line:

```
$ git add file.txt
$ git commit -m "Add file.txt"
$ git log
commit 2a99799c0b9727dc22ae8a790d3978ac40273960 (HEAD -> master)
Author: Johan Abildskov <randomsort@gmail.com>
Date:   Fri Mar 13 13:17:41 2020 +0100
```

What we see in the preceding example is the changeset we add to the stage becomes a part of the next commit we create using the git commit command. The message we pass as an argument is shown in the log. This is useful as we can give a title to each commit, given a reason for a changeset. Many developers also use the message to reference an external issue, maintained in a tool like Jira, GitLab, or Azure DevOps Boards.

If we leave out the -m flag from the commit command, Git will open a text editor in which you can fashion a commit message. This also opens up for using both the subject and body of the commit message. In most corporations, only the subject is used, as additional information is persisted outside of version control. In these situations, put any issue references in the body and leaving them out of the subject. This allows for a cleaner commit header that concisely describes the changes that any Git commit introduces.

In open source workflows, the commit message body is more commonly used to add more documentation on changesets. This information should not duplicate what is written in proper documentation such as READMEs, generated documentation, user instruction, or similar. Rather, it should contain supplementary information relevant for the concrete changeset. The following bullet list is some examples on what could be covered in such documentation:

- The reasoning for introducing this changeset

- Any architectural decisions

- Design choices

- Trade-offs that are not necessarily obvious in the code

- Descriptions of alternative solutions that could be considered

- A slightly more verbose description of the content of the changeset

In Listing 2-1, I've grabbed a commit message out of the Git core source code repository. This shows an example of a commit message using both the subject and body of the commit message.

Listing 2-1. An example commit message with the subject giving a high-level description of the feature and the body verbosely listing the content

```
mm, treewide: rename kzfree() to kfree_sensitive()
```

As said by Linus:
A symmetric naming is only helpful if it implies symmetries in use.
Otherwise it's actively misleading.
In "kzalloc()", the z is meaningful and an important part of what the caller wants.
In "kzfree()", the z is actively detrimental, because maybe in the future we really _might_ want to use that "memfill(0xdeadbeef)" or something. The "zero" part of the interface isn't even _relevant_.
The main reason that kzfree() exists is to clear sensitive information that should not be leaked to other future users of the same memory objects.

In the preceding code, we saw how it can look when we both have a subject and a body in a commit message – in the following code, I will show how it looks when we go through the steps to create a commit without specifying a commit message in the command line.

```
$ git commit
hint: Waiting for your editor to close the file...
[master 1a41582] Commit message from editor
 1 file changed, 0 insertions(+), 0 deletions(-)
 create mode 100644 file2
$ git log -n 1
commit 1a41582591bedad5757914acf3fc8be562e468a4 (HEAD -> master)
Author: Johan Abildskov <randomsort@gmail.com>
Date:    Fri Mar 13 13:19:57 2020 +0100

    Commit message from editor

    This part of the message is written as a part of the message body.
    Notice that there is a newline between the header and the subject.
```

But one step is missing from the previous code that is hard to show in a book. Figure 2-5 shows a screenshot of the editor Git opens on my system with a prepopulated commit message, which we can change to our liking. Note that if there are only empty lines and comments when we save and quit the editor, the commit process will be aborted.

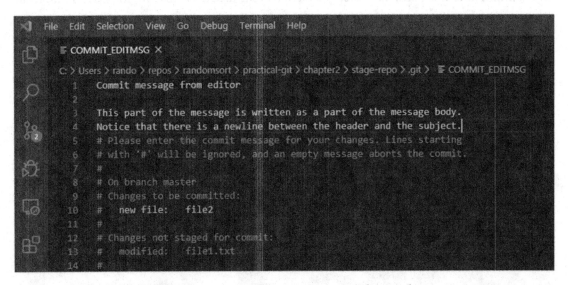

Figure 2-5. *The default view on a commit message editor when no message is specified in the command line*

Out of the box, Git will default to whatever editor your shell is using, defined in the environment variables EDITOR or VISUAL. If Git cannot determine which editor to use, it will fall back to vi, to the dismay of many Windows users. The previously described behavior can be overridden with the configuration core.editor. We will cover configuration later, but be aware that you have the option to choose your favorite editor. It is not necessarily all editors that support being used in this way, or can run by Git without being started with specific configuration. Most commonly used editors are compatible or can be easily configured to work as it should. It is no further away than a Google search that leads to Stack Overflow.

Good, Bad, and UGLY Commit Messages

As we've mentioned earlier, commits are immutable. That also means that commit messages are permanent, and thus it is important to invest some amount of thought in writing them to maximize the value of the message to our collaborators and future self. There is a saying that one of the hard problems in computer science is naming things. I think we can lump in writing commit messages. It is difficult but important.

In this section, we will cover some ground rules for writing good commit messages, some things to avoid, and give examples on both good and bad commit messages.

Before diving into the details, I want to stress that a key factor for useful commit messages is consistency across collaborators in a repository. In my opinion, it is much more important that commit messages have the same semantics and look the same than they are objectively written optimally. It is powerful to be able to skim a list of commits and be able to get a feeling of the life that is going on in the repository. Some also add integrations to their IDEs that decorate each code line with the commit message subject of the commit that most recently changed that code line. This way of working is much more powerful if commit messages have the same basic shape. The Git feature we are using for this is not very sensitively called git blame. It allows us to point fingers at whoever caused a particular change. While this is useful, the connotations on the word blame are not very constructive or conducive of a healthy culture. We will cover git blame at a later point.

The Subject or Header

As can be seen in Figure 2-6, the commit message subject has a prominent position, no matter where you look at it. In the log, it is what we associate with a commit; it is what shows the pulse of our code base through the events they describe. In a repository manager, commonly the files and directories shown are annotated with the commits that last changed them. Some even add these commit messages on a line-per-line basis in their editors. This can, for example, be done using Git lens in Visual Studio Code.

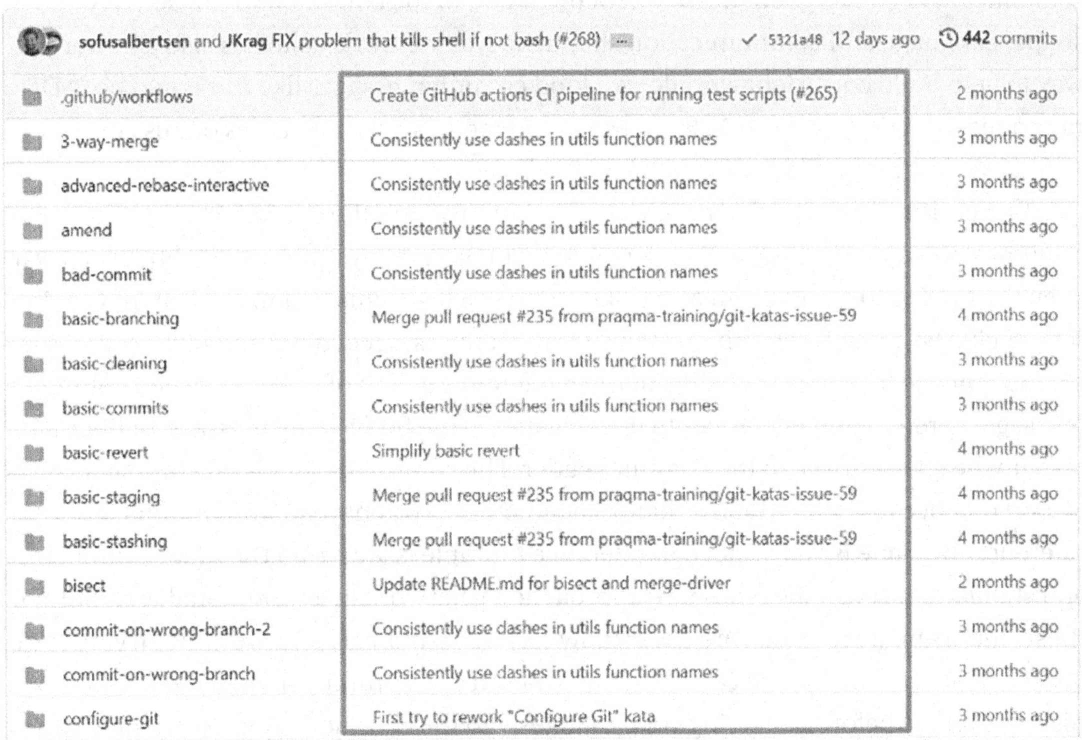

sofusalbertsen and JKrag FIX problem that kills shell if not bash (#268)	✓ 5321a48 12 days ago	🕑 **442** commits
📁 .github/workflows	Create GitHub actions CI pipeline for running test scripts (#265)	2 months ago
📁 3-way-merge	Consistently use dashes in utils function names	3 months ago
📁 advanced-rebase-interactive	Consistently use dashes in utils function names	3 months ago
📁 amend	Consistently use dashes in utils function names	3 months ago
📁 bad-commit	Consistently use dashes in utils function names	3 months ago
📁 basic-branching	Merge pull request #235 from praqma-training/git-katas-issue-59	4 months ago
📁 basic-cleaning	Consistently use dashes in utils function names	3 months ago
📁 basic-commits	Consistently use dashes in utils function names	3 months ago
📁 basic-revert	Simplify basic revert	4 months ago
📁 basic-staging	Merge pull request #235 from praqma-training/git-katas-issue-59	4 months ago
📁 basic-stashing	Merge pull request #235 from praqma-training/git-katas-issue-59	4 months ago
📁 bisect	Update README.md for bisect and merge-driver	2 months ago
📁 commit-on-wrong-branch-2	Consistently use dashes in utils function names	3 months ago
📁 commit-on-wrong-branch	Consistently use dashes in utils function names	3 months ago
📁 configure-git	First try to rework "Configure Git" kata	3 months ago

Figure 2-6. *Commit message headers presented through the GitHub interface*

When most people discuss commit messages, they are simply referring to the subject. There are a few categories of good commit messages, and as mentioned before, it is important that the individual contributors to the code base are aligned on the strategy.

The first strategy that I will cover is simply describing at a high level what has changed in a commit. In my opinion, this should not be describing an implementation detail. Thus, a good commit message could be "Enable separate debug and info logging" or "Move checkout functionality to separate class", while a bad would be "Move checkout() from app.js to checkout.js". My point is that I should be able to get more information than simply the diff from the commit header.

A second style is to describe what will happen if you apply this commit. This can be used successfully in open source projects or on-site where developers contribute to many modules, perhaps some outside of their core responsibilities. Using these semantics also gives a good indication of the intent of the commit and the delivery shape. Language and communication shape the way we work, so this is also a powerful way to help build consistent workflows. Good commit messages like this could be "ADD randomized retries" or "UPDATE prices to 2020 models". Bad examples of this could be "REMOVE unneeded files" or "Add JIRA-1234".

As mentioned previously, many organizations also use the commit header to reference one or more issues. This is a topic that I have many opinions on, but I will try to keep the ranting to a minimum and just introduce a few items to ponder. I am not against referencing issues in a commit message, I think it raises traceability and in most cases is a good practice. I am against using an issue reference in lieu of a proper, useful commit message. I prefer issue references to be relegated to the body of the message rather than take up the sparse space in the commit header. The commit header is one line so it is a good practice to keep it shorter than 70 characters. If you have many commits that reference the same issue, or need to reference multiple issues from the same commit, you should reflect whether you have approached your work in a suboptimal way. Both of these one-to-many relations are a workflow smell and indicate you are either trying to do too much at one time, in the case of many issues in one commit, or are not doing basic history hygiene before delivering your changeset to the common repository. There can of course be all sorts of special scenarios, but in most cases, there should be a one-on-one ratio of commits to issues within a single repository.

A new style has been introduced taking advantage of our more and more advance terminals and emojis getting added to Unicode. Some use these emojis in their commit messages to signal either intent or the type of change. This is sometimes called Gitmojis. In Figure 2-7, you can see examples of both descriptions and usage of some of these.

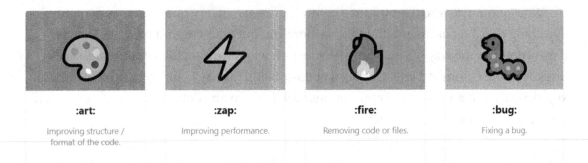

:art:

Improving structure /
format of the code.

:zap:

Improving performance.

:fire:

Removing code or files.

:bug:

Fixing a bug.

Figure 2-7. *Gitmojis used to concisely categorize changesets*

Using the Gitmojis might seem like nothing more than a gimmick, but if used consistently and with thought, it can be a very efficient way of communicating. It takes discipline to use effectively, though. Use the Gitmoji as the very first character in the header if you are using them. Please limit the use of emojis in the commit messages. If nothing else, then make sure that your use of emojis is consistent with the engineering culture of the code base. Emojis that are used for flavor should be added at the end of the commit message, such that they do not interfere with the messaging of the used Gitmoji. Finally, there might be technical challenges depending on how current and customized the tooling that interacts with the repository is. It is possible that either custom tooling or outdated software might not be compatible with emojis in commit messages – or paths for that matter.

The above are some different styles or strategies for writing good commit messages. Which you choose can vary from project to project and from repository to repository. Make sure that there is a high degree of consistency so a git log looks clean! I end this section with a compiled list of bad commit messages that should serve as a warning of how not to write commit messages. The list may or may not be based on actual commit messages:

- Fix typo

- Dummy commit

- Fix CI (on a string of ten commits)

- Maybe this will work

- I don't even know why I *expletive deleted* care anymore

- 🚀 👾 👾 👾 🛸

What should go into the body of a commit message is very project dependent, but if nothing else, I recommend that this is where you put your commit messages – even if this comes in the way of you using the short -m where you set the commit messages directly in the command line. Getting a good-looking history is surely worth those extra keystrokes. I will not cover the commit message body in any detail as there are too many different approaches to cover here.

Recovering from Oops Moments with amend

The command git commit has a flag called amend that allows us to edit the most recent commit. When I say edit, it is a lie. We will cover what happens in more detail later, but as mentioned, commits are immutable, so we don't really edit a commit, we create a new almost identical one, and point to that instead. The old commit does not disappear immediately, but will be garbage collected after some time.

Figure 2-8 shows what happens when we do amend. A new commit is created and the branch pointer updated.

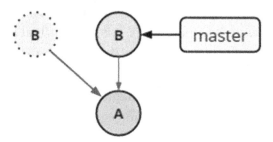

Figure 2-8. *Amending a commit creates a new commit and updates pointers. It leaves a dangling commit that will at some point be garbage collected. The new dangling commit is shown in a faded outline, with the new commit in a full solid line*

There are many scenarios where commit amend is useful. We might have forgot to stage everything that we needed – or staged way too much. We could have written a horrible commit message and immediately regret it. In the following segment, I run through an example of commit and then adding a file to the commit. In the example, I will run the command using -m to specify the message. If we leave the -m out, we will get our $EDITOR opened prepopulated with the message from the commit that we are amending.

```
$ git log -n 2
commit 25cb0925de7cbc8c12803c6d51a7ddbc5f114509 (HEAD -> master)
Author: Johan Abildskov <randomsort@gmail.com>
Date:   Sat Mar 14 13:13:59 2020 +0100

    Add Feature X

commit 67e7eef1a44f222a50207fc20b24477bd9e0ddd8
Author: Johan Abildskov <randomsort@gmail.com>
Date:   Sat Mar 14 13:12:34 2020 +0100

    Initial Commit
$ git add example.md
$ git status
On branch master
Changes to be committed:
  (use "git reset HEAD <file>..." to unstage)

        new file:   example.md

$ git commit –amend -m "ADD Feature X, with docs"
[master 8fb3eba] Add Feature X, with docs
 Date: Sat Mar 14 13:13:59 2020 +0100
 2 files changed, 2 insertions(+)
 create mode 100644 example.md
 create mode 100644 featurex.app

$ git log -n 2
commit 8fb3ebac82ac4940cf478746e04d73eb1882aa76 (HEAD -> master)
Author: Johan Abildskov <randomsort@gmail.com>
Date:   Sat Mar 14 13:13:59 2020 +0100

    Add Feature X, with docs

commit 67e7eef1a44f222a50207fc20b24477bd9e0ddd8
Author: Johan Abildskov <randomsort@gmail.com>
Date:   Sat Mar 14 13:12:34 2020 +0100

    Initial Commit
```

```
$ git status
On branch master
nothing to commit, working tree clean
```

As we can see from the preceding example, we can easily fix a common misstep. While tinkering with the history and commits is generally considered bad practice, this is only on items that are shared between people. So as long as we are working on commits that are not shared, we should take the care to actively edit and fashion our history so it provides as much value as possible for posterity.

Getting Clean Commits with .gitignore

A common mistake for developers is to add too much into their commits. This could be compiled files, logs, or other build artifacts. If we are building Python code, we would never be interested in persisting the .pyc compiled Python files as part of our versioned source code. Getting too much into our repositories can have a few unfortunate outcomes.

First, it can degrade performance over time. Both doing the initial clone and getting different commits into the workspace with checkout can become long-running tasks. As Git is immutable and distributed, this can have a high price and be tough to fix later.

Second, it obfuscates the real changes and makes it more difficult to make commits that have a well-defined boundary and obvious changeset. If a commit contains changes on tens of thousands of files due to a bunch of changed build artifacts, it can be very difficult to discern where the real logical change is buried.

Third, it enforces bad habits just adding all that has changed into the next commit. As professional software workers, we must take care and ensure what we deliver is what we intend to deliver. In that manner, simply adding what is present in our repository does help us forming deliberate changeset.

Fortunately, Git comes with a solution that can help us avoid accidentally cluttering up our repositories. Git comes with a feature that allows us to put paths into a file called .gitignore, and files contained in here will be ignored when we stage items for committing. This allows us to be more liberal when we stage content. Using git add folder/ is much more efficient than individually staging files.

A .gitignore file contains a list of patterns to be ignored. If you prefix a line with an exclamation point, that pattern will be included, even if it previously has been ignored. In the following figures, we will show what will be staged depending on the .gitignore file.

Listing 2-2 shows an example .gitignore file that will work well for Python projects.

Listing 2-2. A basic .gitignore file that can be used for Python projects to avoid cluttering the repository (generated from `https://gitignore.io`)

```
# Created by www.gitignore.io/api/python
# Edit at www.gitignore.io/?templates=python

### Python ###
# Byte-compiled / optimized / DLL files
__pycache__/
*.py[cod]
*$py.class

# C extensions
*.so
```

Note   For example .gitignore files for most commonly used languages and frameworks, you can go to gitignore.io and download a suitable one.

After adding a .gitignore file to our repository, we might still have some cleanup to do. Just because we have ignored files does not remove already committed files from the workspace. More importantly, it does not remove them from the history, so they still take up space, even though they no longer clutter the workspace. How to handle this is an entirely different and complex beast that we will attack later on.

In the following command-line snippet, you can see how adding a .gitignore file changes the behavior of the add command:

```
$ ls
app.exe* example.md  featurex.app  file
$ git add .
$ git status
 $ git status
```

```
On branch master
Changes to be committed:
  (use "git reset HEAD <file>..." to unstage)

        new file:    app.exe

$ git restore app.exe

$ git status
On branch master
Untracked files:
  (use "git add <file>..." to include in what will be committed)

        app.exe

nothing added to commit but untracked files present (use "git add" to
track)
$ echo "*.exe" > .gitignore
$ git add .
$ git status
On branch master
Changes to be committed:
  (use "git reset HEAD <file>..." to unstage)

        new file:    .gitignore
```

As can be seen from the preceding sample, creating a .gitignore file helps keep our repository from getting unnecessarily cluttered. We can also see that the .gitignore file is simply a file, and changes to it will be tracked just like any other file changes.

Advanced .gitignore

While the preceding example is quite nice and provides a lot of value, it is often not enough. We tend to have more elaborate schemes for what is allowable inside of our repository.

It is not uncommon to make schemes such as "We will not allow pngs in our repository except for inside the folder images". We can do such things with the git ignore file.

A git ignore file contains a list of patterns that are applied from top to bottom. We can prefix lines with a ! to make them an inclusion rather than an exclusion.

Thus, to obtain the preceding scenario, we can use the following .gitignore file. Note that lines inside the git ignore file that starts with a # are ignored.

```
# Example .gitignore
# Exclude all pngs
*.png
# Include pngs in images/
!images/*.png
```

BUILDING A .GITIGNORE FILE

The following set of commands builds a git ignore file in the command line that will disallow png files from being added to the repository, except if they are in the images folder.

First, we notice that there are two png files in the repository, one in the root and one in the images folder. When we then add the root (.), both png files are staged.

```
$ ls
file.png  images/  README.md
$ git add .

$ git status
On branch master
Changes to be committed:
  (use "git reset HEAD <file>..." to unstage)

        new file:   file.png
        new file:   images/file.png
$ git restore .
$ git status
On branch master
Untracked files:
  (use "git add <file>..." to include in what will be committed)

        file.png
        images/file.png
```

```
nothing added to commit but untracked files present (use "git add" to track)
```

After having restored our stage to the state that is in the repository, we ignore png files completely in our repository. When we then stage the root, no png files are staged.

```
$ echo *.png > .gitignore
$ git add .
$ git status
On branch master
Changes to be committed:
  (use "git reset HEAD <file>..." to unstage)

        new file:   .gitignore

$ git restore .
$ git status
On branch master
Untracked files:
  (use "git add <file>..." to include in what will be committed)

        .gitignore

nothing added to commit but untracked files present (use "git add" to track)
```

Now that we've again restore to the basic state, we can add an exception to the preceding rule using the ! as a prefix to the pattern. In this case, we allow pngs inside of the images folder.

```
$ echo !images/*.png >> .gitignore
$ git add .
$ git status
On branch master
Changes to be committed:
  (use "git reset HEAD <file>..." to unstage)

        new file:   .gitignore
        new file:   images/file.png
```

This could also have been achieved with a separate .gitignore file inside of the images folder containing only the line !*.png. This would have the effect to saying, in this folder and the following png files are allowed no matter what the repository otherwise believes. Thus, we can have an arbitrary amount of git ignore files placed around in our directory structure. As with many other aspects of Git, this adds complexity, and we should be disciplined around adding ignore files outside of the root.

Globbing git ignore

In shell languages, there is a concept of globbing, which is a kind of fuzzy wildcard expansion. An * represents any single name. But we can also use the sequence ** to represent arbitrary nesting. This allows us to say things like "We do not want png files in our repository, unless they are in a folder called images, no matter where that folder is". This can be useful in a scenario where you would like to permit png files in the repository, but you worry that people will accidentally add pngs that they have randomly lying around. Saying pngs are allowed if they are put in a folder called images forces developers to be more deliberate about adding pngs to the repository, while not being overly restrictive.

The following examples start from the previous exercise and then open up for a few more locations.

GLOB PATTERNS IN GIT IGNORE

This exercise assumes we have the same git ignore file that we closed the last exercise with, that is, a git ignore file denying pngs except for the folder images/ in the root of the repository. This means that we have a few different images folders that will not have their content allowed.

We start from the setup we had in the last exercise and then add a wildcard pattern to the gitignore file.

```
$ echo '!*/images/*.png' >> .gitignore
$ git add .
$ git status
$ git status
On branch master
Changes to be committed:
  (use "git reset HEAD <file>..." to unstage)

        new file:   .gitignore
        new file:   images/file.png
        new file:   subfolder/images/file.png

$ git restore .
```

We have now added a wildcard pattern that allows any subfolder to have pngs in a subfolder called images. This allows us to more broadly let exceptions without doing everything on a folder-by-folder level.

```
$ echo '!**/images/*.png' >> .gitignore
$ git add .
$ git status
On branch master
Changes to be committed:
  (use "git reset HEAD <file>..." to unstage)

        new file:   .gitignore
        new file:   images/file.png
        new file:   subfolder/images/file.png
        new file:   subfolder/subfolder/images/file.png
```

We have now added an even broader pattern stating that as long as pngs are in a folder called images/, it doesn't matter how far down the directory tree this happens. This clause is more broad than the first in this exercise, so we can go back and delete the line !*/images/*.png from the Git ignore file as this is covered by the line just added.

The preceding examples show very concretely how we can create elaborate schemes that will give us fine-grained control over what goes into the repository. It also shows that it quickly can become complex, even with such a simple example as the one earlier.

I highly recommend against creating too complex gitignore files, they can quickly become seemingly magical, and it stops being obvious to the developer what is going on when they are using their version control system. This is of course to be avoided if possible.

Git Katas

In order to support the learning goals of this chapter best, I recommend that you go through the following Git katas:

- basic-commits

- basic-staging

- amend

- ignore

Summary

In this chapter, we have covered the stage and how we can use that to create beautiful atomic commits. We have also discussed commit messages and how to write them well. More importantly, we discussed a few different strategies for how to decide what patterns you want your commit messages to follow. We touched on the simplest way of redoing a commit, using amend. Finally, we discussed how we can use the Git ignore file to avoid unintentional files in our repository. Armed with this knowledge, we are ready to venture forth and create a long history of perfect commits.

CHAPTER 3

Linear History

Git is famously known for its lightweight branches. They are highly performant both in terms of creation and merging. They are also relatively simple to use as a developer. Anyone who has been in a seemingly unresolvable merge conflict will contest this statement.

In short, branches are how we manage our source code life cycle, how we manage different versions of our code base, and how we isolate our changesets to facilitate atomic changes and collaboration.

Branches can seem a bit complex, but I will do my best to give you the right vocabulary and mental model to be able to wield branches with ease.

In this chapter, we are going to cover a linear history, that is, repositories with an unbroken, single-string chain of commits. First, we will cover the basic building blocks for Git's branching model. Then, we will show how they interact in a visual way and round off with how this comes to fruition through tasks in a Git repository.

Branching Foundations

When we think of branches, two things spring into mind. One is divergence. It even shows in natural language. "The road branched" refers to a road splitting into multiple directions. Secondly, our intuition of a branch is something that has some length – not just a single point. In terms of version control, we would then expect that we have branches when we have separate chains of commits. This intuition is the root of much confusion when people learn Git. In Figure 3-1, we can see how these concepts map into a drawing of an actual tree.

© Johan Abildskov 2020
J. Abildskov, *Practical Git*, https://doi.org/10.1007/978-1-4842-6270-2_3

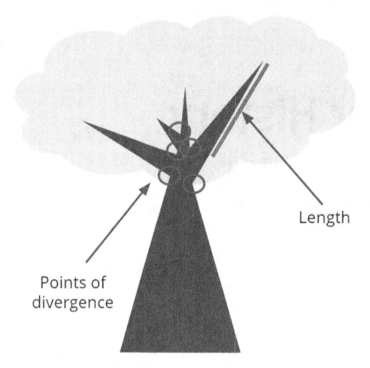

Figure 3-1. *Our intuition is shown; that branches have lengths and represent points of divergence*

In Git, a branch is nothing more than a reference to a single commit. This is the single most important statement in this book, so I will repeat it. In Git, a branch is nothing more than a reference to a single commit. This means that when we mention a branch of our source code, we usually refer to the newest commit on that branch and the commits that precede it. But technically, the branch is simply pointing to the newest commit, and the rest of the commits "on the branch" are derived by following the parent pointer from this commit. This also means that there is not necessarily any divergence needed for branches to exist. We can have two branches that point to the same commit and thus two branches that are identical without any divergence.

This layout is shown in Figure 3-2. We have a string of commits and three branches pointing into this string of commits. Branches A and B point to the same commit, while branch C points to a different commit. Note that while C is different from A and B, there is no divergence. C is simply a prefix of A and B. This will become important later when we talk about merges.

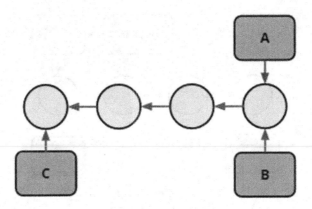

Figure 3-2. *Three branches in a linear history. A and B point to the same commit, while C points to a predecessor of A and B*

Keeping Track of Your HEAD

As described earlier, we can have multiple branches in the same repository and even pointing to the same commit. This makes it nonobvious what branch we are currently working on. In Git, the branch that is currently active is said to be checked out. Git uses a file called HEAD to keep track of what is currently checked out.

In Figure 3-3, you can see how the HEAD pointer references a branch pointer that is moving while we create commits.

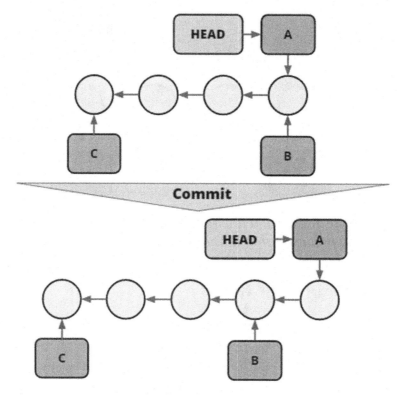

Figure 3-3. *How the branch moves*

What HEAD is pointing at defines two things. First, HEAD points to a branch, that is, the branch that moves as we make more commits. Second, it is the commit that our workspace and stage are compared to when we use commands like git status.

Committing on Your Branches

From the previous chapter, we know how to create commits. And we have now covered a branch pointer and the HEAD pointer also. This means we are now ready to create a few commits on our master branch. An important point to note, as we commit, is that the HEAD pointer does not change. It keeps pointing to the master branch, and what the master branch points at changes.

The following exercise will go through the scenario in Figure 3-3 with git commands.

COMMITTING

In the following exercise, we will first see that our history matches that of Figure 3-3. Then we will make a commit and see that our history now matches the bottom half of Figure 3-3. This exercise can be found in the source code for this book.

```
$ git log --oneline
f157eed (HEAD -> A, B) 4
3652176 3
5cbbdc1 (C) 2
6856025 1

$ echo 5 > README.md

$ git commit -am "5"
[A 933a6c5] 5
 1 file changed, 1 insertion(+), 1 deletion(-)

$ git log --oneline
933a6c5 (HEAD -> A) 5
f157eed (B) 4
3652176 3
5cbbdc1 (C) 2
6856025 1
```

As could be seen in the following exercise, we move a branch when we create commits, yet the HEAD remains unchanged.

Checking Out a Previous Version

So far, we have only concerned ourselves with creating commits. We have not been navigating history actively. In this section, I will show you how you can switch between versions in your workspace. A key feature of Git is that it is fast. This also means that making your workspace resemble a different version of your code base is a trivial task. As Git is distributed, we have the entirety of the repository represented locally, which also allows these operations to happen, even if we are offline.

We use the command `git checkout <target>` to put a specific revision in our workspace. As target checkout can grab anything that ends up in resolving a commit. Most commonly, we use branches, tags, or commit shas. Git checkout is a two-step process. First, it moves the HEAD pointer to the specific revision. Then, it takes what content is in that revision and moves it into the workspace, to make the workspace look like that revision. If Git is unable to do this in a safe manner, it will abort the checkout. That means that if you have work that would be overwritten by the checkout, Git will not complete the operation. Git will also not clean up any files lying around untracked. If we use a tag or a commit sha as the target for the checkout command, we will end up in a detached HEAD state. This sounds more dangerous than it is. It simply means that we are not currently tracking any branch and potentially we can lose the work that we do in this point as we are not committing on any branch. There is however no reason to worry about this. Later, we will solve exactly this issue together.

In the following exercise, we will see how we can switch between different versions of repository using the command git checkout. We will check out separate commits, see how the workspace changes, and get back to the most recent version.

CHECKING OUT DIFFERENT VERSIONS

This exercise starts with the end state of the previous exercise.

```
$ git log --oneline --decorate
7f1c255 (HEAD -> A) 5
f157eed (B) 4
3652176 3
5cbbdc1 (C) 2
6856025 1

$ cat README.md
5

$ git checkout 4
error: pathspec '4' did not match any file(s) known to git.

$ git checkout B
Switched to branch 'B'
```

```
$ cat README.md
4

$ git log --oneline --decorate
f157eed (HEAD -> B) 4
3652176 3
5cbbdc1 (C) 2
6856025 1

$ git checkout C
Switched to branch 'C'

$ cat README.md
2

$ git checkout A
Switched to branch 'A'

$ cat README.md
5

$ echo "Important information" > README.md

$ git checkout B
error: Your local changes to the following files would be overwritten by
checkout:
        README.md
Please commit your changes or stash them before you switch branches.
Aborting
```

Notice that when we try to check out something that will overwrite changes in our workspace in an unsafe way, Git will prevent that action and will advise on possible actions.

When you run through the preceding exercise, notice how quick each operation is. It barely takes any time at all. While this is a small and trivial repository, similar performance can be seen on even quite large repositories. Simply the fact that Git does not need to communicate with a server is a big advantage, even assuming the best conditions on network connectivity and server load.

Seeing the Diff Between Different Versions

In the previous section, we saw how we could instantiate any version of our code base into our workspace. With this knowledge, a common way to figure out what the difference between two versions of our repository is is to have two copies of the same repository on disk, check out the different versions in the different folders, and compare them. This can either be done by hand, investigating areas of interest, or be done using a tool to show the difference. This is not idiomatic Git. It is also error prone and can lead to tedious rework, as you repeatedly check which version was in which folder and try to figure out which file to copy where.

Git solves this with the diff command. The diff command shows the difference between two commits. The command takes two commits, or references to commits as arguments. If only one argument is given, HEAD is assumed for the first argument. The command then looks like this: git diff <commit1> <commit2>, and an example could be git diff master release-1.0. This will then show what content wise is the difference between the commit master refers to and the commit that release-1.0 refers to.

Note   The order of the arguments to git diff matters. A file creation in one direction becomes a file deletion if you switch the order of the arguments. 20 lines added becomes 20 lines removed. This can potentially lead to confusion when you try to figure out what went into a changeset.

My intuition around diff is that I point Git to two different commits, and it will tell me what I would have to do to go from one to the other. This can of course also be seen as what has happened between the two. In Listing 3-1, this is shown, as well as the impact of the order of the arguments to diff.

Listing 3-1. A diff and the impact of the order of the arguments. Here, we need to delete a 2 and add a 5 or, in the other direction, delete a 5 and add a 2

```
$ git diff C A
diff --git a/README.md b/README.md
index 0cfbf08..7edff8 100644
--- a/README.md
+++ b/README.md
```

```
@@ -1 +1 @@
-2
+5

$ git diff C A
diff --git b/README.md a/README.md
index 7edff8..0cfbf08 100644
--- a/README.md
+++ b/README.md
@@ -1 +1 @@
-5

+2
```

The diff command does not pay any attention to the history between the commits, whether that is diverging or not. Git simply tells you what the difference is between the two workspaces represented by the commits you pass as arguments.

Sometimes, patch output can be a bit difficult to parse – in particular, small changes in long lines. This can sometimes be helped with the flag --word-diff, which will inline the change in the line rather than as two separate lines. This can be seen in Listing 3-2.

Listing 3-2. Showing how it is much easier to see what the changes are using the --word-diff flag. This can vary from use case to use case

```
Normal Diff
 <Navbar bg="success" variant="dark">
-      <Navbar.Brand href={window.location.host}>Cultooling</Navbar.Brand>
+      <Navbar.Brand href={homeUrl()}>Cultooling</Navbar.Brand>
       <Nav className="mr-auto">
-        <Nav.Link href={window.location.host}>Home</Nav.Link>
+        <Nav.Link href={homeUrl()}>Home</Nav.Link>
       </Nav>
    </Navbar>
With --word-diff
<Navbar bg="success" variant="dark">
    <Navbar.Brand
```

```
[-href={window.location.host}>Cultooling</Navbar.Brand>-]
{+href={homeUrl()}>Cultooling</Navbar.Brand>+}
    <Nav className="mr-auto">
      <Nav.Link
[-href={window.location.host}>Home</Nav.Link>-]{+href={homeUrl()}>Home
</Nav.Link>+}
    </Nav>
  </Navbar>
```

We can also use the diff command without arguments or with the flag `--staged` to see the difference between our workspace, stage, and repository. These two commands are strong as tools that will help you become more deliberate about the commits you make.

Git Katas

In order to support the learning goals of this chapter, I urge you to go and solve the following Git katas:

- Detached HEAD.

- It can be useful to also do the basic-commits again and pay attention to the branch-specific things going on.

Summary

In this chapter, we first covered using a simple branch including the HEAD pointer that keeps track of what we currently have checked out. We also created a few commits and saw our branch pointer move as we did so. Afterward, we moved through our history with the checkout command and rounded off with some diff magic, showing us exactly what happens between two points in history. After this chapter, you should feel comfortable working with a linear branch history.

CHAPTER 4

Complex Branching

In the last chapter, we looked at a linear history. This can be fine for trivial repositories, but if we are confident working with branches, it will introduce almost no overhead, so we can wield the power of branches, even for our simplest projects.

There are many benefits from working actively with branches in Git. We will cover collaboration with multiple developers in the next chapter, but even for a solo developer, there are wins from branches. They primarily derive from the fact that we can use branches to isolate our work. When we isolate our work, we can mitigate some of the cost of multitasking. By isolating our work on a branch, we can always create a new branch, should an urgent task need to be developed. We can safely run experiments on a branch and only integrate our experiment if it comes out in a favorable way. As mentioned before, branches are a great cause of confusion around how Git works. This is very unfortunate as they are the key to both gaining the full value of Git and understanding many concepts including working with remote repositories and all but the simplest collaboration schemes.

In this chapter, we will focus on getting a healthy mental model around multiple branches and get enough hands-on experience that you will be able to use and reason about branches.

Creating Branches

We have covered that a branch is a pointer to a commit. Concretely, that means that a branch is a file in the repository containing the sha to the commit the branch points at. This can be seen in Listing 4-1.

Listing 4-1. A branch is a file containing the sha of the commit it points to

```
$ cat .git/refs/heads/master
5355b7b7f01b6d69c1ae94b428f54952139eb2f8
$ git log --oneline --decorate -n 1
5355b7b (HEAD -> master, origin/master, origin/HEAD) [Chapter 7] Add
aliases exercise
```

© Johan Abildskov 2020
J. Abildskov, *Practical Git*, https://doi.org/10.1007/978-1-4842-6270-2_4

We can use the command git branch to manipulate and list branches. There are subtleties when it comes to remote branches, but we will cover those in the next chapter. When we use the command without arguments, we list the (local) branches.

We also create branches using the branch command. We call with two arguments: git branch <branch-name> <commit>. As an example: git branch my-branch master. This will create a branch in the repository. It will be called my-branch and point to the same commit as master. This can be seen in Figure 4-1.

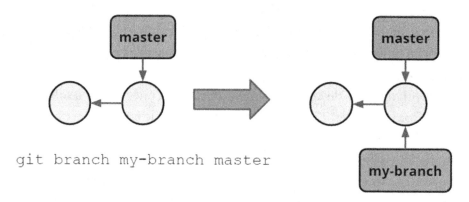

Figure 4-1. *Creating a branch from a reference*

Now that we have created a branch, we can do some work on the different branches. Depending on what HEAD currently is pointing at, new commits will be created at an appropriate location, with the currently checked-out branch updated to point at the new commit. This can be seen in Figure 4-2.

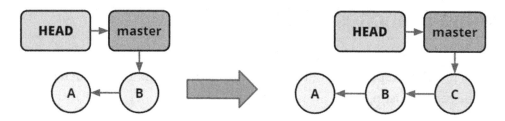

Figure 4-2. *Creating commits on a branch will add the commit and update the branch pointer*

Now that we have seen how it looks when we create commits on branches, we are ready for the next step in branching

Working with Multiple Branches

In Git, it really does not make any sense to work without any branches, and we are by default always working on one branch: the master branch. But the true power comes from juggling multiple branches. There are two primary tasks when working with multiple branches. One is keeping our work separate on different branches. We have covered that earlier. The other part is getting changes made on multiple branches into the same branch. This is commonly referred to as merging. There are multiple ways to do this. In this chapter, we are going to cover merging and rebasing.

Conceptually, when we want to merge two branches, we create a new commit containing the joint changeset from the two branches. This works by finding the point at which the branches diverged and joining the two changesets. This can be seen in Figure 4-3.

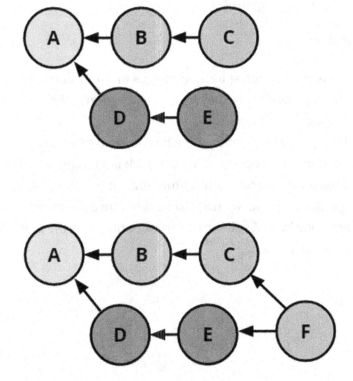

Figure 4-3. *A common merge, merging the branches pointing to C and E, respectively*

In the case that the changesets are compatible, Git will handle everything for us. If the changesets are not compatible, or Git fails to merge them, we will end up in a merge conflict. We will cover these later in this chapter. In most code bases I've been working with, merge conflicts have been uncommon.

Merge

Merging is another place where our language can come in the way of our understanding of Git. We both talk about the abstract merging of branches, disregarding how we intend to do this, and we talk about the command `git merge`.

The common way to use the merge command is with the form `git merge branch` which will merge the changeset from branch into the branch currently checked out, for example, `git merge feature-123`. There are other options, but I like this way of working as we then only change the branch that we are on, which is good as it leads to relatively few issues. This merge is how Figure 4-3 was created.

Fast-Forward Merges

Fast-forward merges are the simplest form of merges in Git. Unfortunately, there is also a bit of misunderstanding around how they work. This section will hopefully leave you in a state where you love fast-forward merges.

A fast-forward merge happens when there has been no divergence between the branches you are merging. This occurs when a branch is a continuation of another. In Figure 4-4, we can see this scenario as the feature branch is linearly ahead of master. To merge the change in feature, all we need to do is to move the master branch pointer to the commit feature points at. As all the changes contained in the master branch are already part of the feature branch.

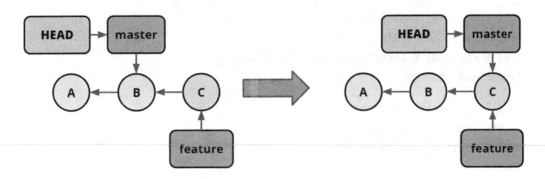

`git branch merge feature`

Figure 4-4. *Doing a fast-forward merge does not result in any new commits, but is a simple operation*

This also means that there is no possibility for any conflict doing a fast-forward merge. For this reason, fast-forward merges can be considered safe.

Note   Some workflows use a Git feature where a new commit is created to mark the merge of a branch. This creates a merge commit, without a changeset, to mark that at this point the branches were merged. This is done with the command git merge --no-ff <branch>.

FAST FORWARD

In this exercise, we are going to start with only the master branch. It has two commits on it. We are going to create a branch called feature, create a commit, and merge that into master. This exercise can be found in the exercise folder as chapter4/fast-forward/.

```
$ git log --oneline --decorate
fa8d7db (HEAD -> master) second commit
35b6a68 Initial Commit

$ git checkout -b feature
Switched to a new branch 'feature'

$ git add 1.txt
```

```
$ git commit -m "Adding file1"
[feature 4b346fe] Adding file1
 1 file changed, 0 insertions(+), 0 deletions(-)
 create mode 100644 1.txt

$ git log --oneline --decorate
4b346fe (HEAD -> feature) Adding file1
fa8d7db (master) second commit
35b6a68 Initial Commit
```

At this point, the feature branch contains a commit that is not on master, but master contains nothing that is not also reachable from the feature branch.

```
$ git checkout master
Switched to branch 'master'

$ git merge feature
Updating fa8d7db..4b346fe
Fast-forward
 1.txt | 0
 1 file changed, 0 insertions(+), 0 deletions(-)
 create mode 100644 1.txt
```

Git tells us it is doing a fast-forward and from which commit it moves the pointer.

```
$ git log --oneline
4b346fe (HEAD -> master, feature) Adding file1
fa8d7db second commit
35b6a68 Initial Commit
```

If we compare this out with the one from the log statement before the fast-forward merge, we can see the commit ID is identical. This means that no new commit has been created and the change has been purely a branch update.

As can be seen from the preceding exercise, fast-forward merges by default do not result in new commits. This means that this type of merges is a very quick operation as it is simply a two-step procedure: write updated sha to the branch file, and then check out the workspace at that revision.

Three-Way Merges

In the previous section, we covered trivial or fast-forward merges, where there are no divergence and no possibility of conflicts. In this section, we will treat the plain merge or the three-way merge. These occur when both of the branches that we are merging contain work that is only on one branch. This divergence is wholly natural and happens in most situations where multiple developers are collaborating on a single source base. Commonly, what happens is that while we were developing on our feature branch, some other developer has delivered some changes to the master branch. As such, the point at which we branched out from the master branch is no longer the newest commit on the master branch. As commits represent a specific state of the workspace, we need to create a new commit that contains the state of the workspace after grabbing both changesets. In Figure 4-5, you can see how this looks on the Git graph before and after a merge. In the next exercise, we will cover how it looks on disk.

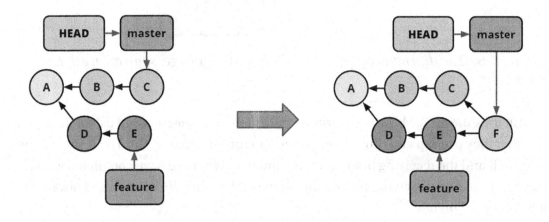

```
git branch merge feature
```

Figure 4-5. *Merging two branches creates a new commit and updates a branch pointer*

Three-way merges are named as such because three points are involved in the merge – both end states as well as the point from which both branches depart. We name these the source, target, and merge base, respectively. This can be seen in Figure 4-6.

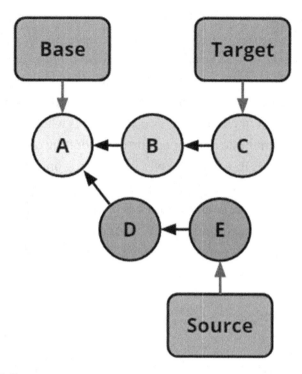

Figure 4-6. *The different components of a three-way merge: source, target, and merge base*

Git uses the merge base to determine the different changesets and calculate whether they overlap and thus cannot be automatically fused by Git. The result will be a commit and the receiving branch will be updated. When we have completed a three-way merge in one direction, if we do the merge in the other direction, it will always be a fast-forward merge.

THREE-WAY MERGE

In this exercise, we have two branches with different content that we like to merge. We will first merge the content from master into feature. Then, we will update the master to the feature branch. This is a common workflow as you can first test out the end state in your feature branch before delivering to master. The repository for this exercise can be found in the exercises as chapter4/three-way-merge/.

```
$ git log --all --graph --oneline
* d03b0bd (HEAD -> feature) Add feature.txt
| * 390d440 (master) Add master.txt
|/
* ea2b9f5 second commit
* f90da57 Initial Commit
```

We see that we have two branches that have diverged.

```
$ git merge master
Merge made by the 'recursive' strategy.
 master.txt | 0
 1 file changed, 0 insertions(+), 0 deletions(-)
 create mode 100644 master.txt
```

When we merge the changes from master into the feature branch, the merge is solved using the three-way merge. It is using the recursive strategy which is an implementation detail we can safely ignore.

```
$ git log --all --graph --oneline
*   ddeeef9 (HEAD -> feature) Merge branch 'master' into feature
|\
| * 390d440 (master) Add master.txt
* | d03b0bd Add feature.txt
|/
* ea2b9f5 second commit
* f90da57 Initial Commit
```

The three-way merge led to a new commit ddeeef9. Note that the master branch still points at the same commit it did before.

```
$ git checkout master
Switched to branch 'master'
```

```
$ git merge feature
Updating 390d440..ddeeef9
Fast-forward
 feature.txt | 0
 1 file changed, 0 insertions(+), 0 deletions(-)
 create mode 100644 feature.txt
```

Now that we merge the branches in the other direction, we get a fast-forward merge. This is true because all the content reachable from master is also reachable from feature, and Git thus considers this merge already solved. Many workflows only allow fast-forward merges on master, and this is how to achieve it.

```
$ git log --all --graph --oneline
*   ddeeef9 (HEAD -> master, feature) Merge branch 'master' into feature
|\
| * 390d440 Add master.txt
* | d03b0bd Add feature.txt
|/
* ea2b9f5 second commit
* f90da57 Initial Commit
```

In the preceding code, we walked through a three-way merge and noticed that repeating a three-way merge in the other direction caused a fast-forward merge.

The preceding exercise went through the happy path scenario. When our merges are simple, Git can easily resolve them automatically and we feel powerful. Unfortunately, it is not always the case that Git can resolve merges for us. We cover this in the next section.

Merge Conflicts

It can be the case that Git is unable to determine what the result should be from merging branches. In this case, Git will ask for the user to resolve the merge and resume the process. This situation is called a merge conflict. Git will drop to the prompt and mark files as being in a state of conflict. Listing 4-2 shows this through a status command.

Listing 4-2. Git status shows that we are in a state of an unresolved merge conflict and instructs as to what our next steps are

```
$ git status
On branch master
You have unmerged paths.
  (fix conflicts and run "git commit")
  (use "git merge --abort" to abort the merge)
```

```
Unmerged paths:
  (use "git add <file>..." to mark resolution)
        both modified:    mergesort.py
no changes added to commit (use "git add" and/or "git commit -a")
```

The simplest way that I can explain how to resolve a merge conflict is you need to make the workspace look like you want the merge to be and then tell Git that you are done. Git outputs so-called markers in the conflicted files. This can be seen in Listing 4-3.

Listing 4-3. Merge markers in a file show origin of different changes

```
$ cat mergesort.py
from heapq import merge

def merge_sort2(m):
    """Sort list, using two part merge sort"""
    if len(m) <= 1:
        return m

    # Determine the pivot point
    middle = len(m) // 2

    # Split the list at the pivot
<<<<<<< HEAD
    left = m[:middle]
    right = m[middle:]
=======
    right = m[middle:]
    left = m[:middle]
>>>>>>> Mergesort-Impl
<Rest of file truncated>
```

If you encounter complex merge conflicts, often it helps to use an external merge tool such as meld or kdiff. Under normal circumstances must merge conflicts are simple to resolve and can simply be handled in your normal editor. Editors, such as Visual Studio Code, understand the markers that Git put in your files and this makes it easier to resolve the merge conflict.

There can be multiple merge conflicts in the same file. Git looks at smaller chunks, to figure out similarities between versions of files. This makes it easier to handle merge conflicts as you do not have to decide on an entire file in one go, but rather can decompose into smaller segments to compare.

MERGE CONFLICT

In this exercise, we will go through the same situation as in the previous exercise except that the diverging branches will have noncompatible changes. This will lead to a merge conflict that we will resolve. This exercise can be found in the examples under chapter4/merge-conflict/.

```
$ ls
0.txt  master.txt

$ cat master.txt
feature

$ git log --oneline --decorate --graph --all
* 6ce4209 (HEAD -> feature) Add feature.txt
| * c301b9a (master) Add master.txt
|/
* f237b8b second commit
* 7e48076 Initial Commit

$ git checkout master
Switched to branch 'master'

$ cat master.txt
master
```

Now, we have gotten our bearing in the repository. Two branches have diverged. Each has added the file master.txt with different content.

```
$ git merge feature
Auto-merging master.txt
CONFLICT (add/add): Merge conflict in master.txt
Automatic merge failed; fix conflicts and then commit the result.
```

After we initiate the merge, Git detects the merge conflict and pauses the merge, prompting us to resolve the merge.

```
$ git status
On branch master
You have unmerged paths.
  (fix conflicts and run "git commit")
  (use "git merge --abort" to abort the merge)

Unmerged paths:
  (use "git add <file>..." to mark resolution)

        both added:        master.txt

no changes added to commit (use "git add" and/or "git commit -a")
```

Using git status to show us where we have problems, lets us know that Git was unable to merge the file master.txt.

```
$ cat master.txt
<<<<<<< HEAD
master
=======
feature
>>>>>>> feature
```

Git has put merge markers showing the different changesets in master.txt. This shows that the current state is the file containing master and the incoming change is the file containing feature.

```
$ echo master > master.txt
```

```
$ git add master.txt
warning: LF will be replaced by CRLF in master.txt.
The file will have its original line endings in your working directory.
```

Most often, we want to complete the merge inside of our editor or merge tool, but in this case, I simply select the state that I want. Note that this state can be either of the solutions or some combination of them. This is why Git needs human intervention – it is unaware of the semantics of our source. We use add to mark the file as being in a resolved state.

```
$ git status
On branch master
All conflicts fixed but you are still merging.
  (use "git commit" to conclude merge)
```

```
$ git commit
[master 3be77eb] Merge branch 'feature'

$ git log --oneline --decorate --graph --all
*   3be77eb (HEAD -> master) Merge branch 'feature'
|\
| * 6ce4209 (feature) Add feature.txt
* | c301b9a Add master.txt
|/
* f237b8b second commit
* 7e48076 Initial Commit
```

Having resolved the merge conflict, we see we are in a similar situation as the happy path three-way merge. We just had to help Git a little bit along the way.

As can be seen in this exercise, it is not a daunting task to resolve a merge conflict. It can however be difficult in complex scenarios and when working with a code base that we are not comfortable with.

Rebase

An alternative to the three-way merge is the rebase. In contrast to the three-way merge that creates a new commit representing the workspace resulting from merging two branches, the rebase intuitively moves the commits. This is technically wrong, but we'll keep the intuition for now. When we rebase our branch on top of another branch, intuitively we move the commits on our branch and apply them on top of the target branch. This can be seen in Figure 4-7.

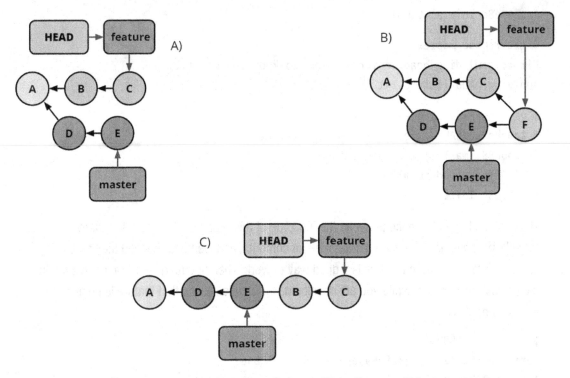

Figure 4-7. *Rebase vs. merge. Starting from A, B is the result from merging master to feature, while C is the result of rebasing feature onto master*

We use the `git rebase <target>` command to rebase HEAD on top of `<target>`. Assuming feature is checked out, we would write `git rebase master` to rebase the feature branch on top of master. This can be seen in Figure 4-7(c).

REBASE EXERCISE

In this exercise, we start with the same situation as we do in the three-way-merge exercise, but instead of merging the branches, we are going to rebase `feature` on top of `master` instead. The repository can be found in the exercise folder as `chapter4/rebase/`.

```
$ git log --oneline --graph --all
* b188294 (HEAD -> feature) Add feature.txt
| * 8cab888 (master) Add master.txt
|/
* 6fb6ffc second commit
```

```
* 2a97e8c Initial Commit

$ git rebase master
First, rewinding head to replay your work on top of it...
Applying: Add feature.txt

$ git log --oneline --graph --all
* 449abd2 (HEAD -> feature) Add feature.txt
* 8cab888 (master) Add master.txt
* 6fb6ffc second commit
* 2a97e8c Initial Commit
```

There is one huge difference between the outcome of this rebase, rather than the merge. Namely, we have not increased the amounts of commits, and we have reduced the complexity of the Git graph. In particular, this is a good way to work when updating your branch to contain the newest from master while you are developing your code. Notice that feature is pointing to a new commit sha.

```
$ git show b18829
commit b1882942ed4722828d595e3428fbac75522bb587
Author: Johan Abildskov <randomsort@gmail.com>
Date:   Mon May 4 09:34:52 2020 +0200

    Add feature.txt

diff --git a/feature.txt b/feature.txt
new file mode 100644
index 0000000..e69de29
```

Here, we use show to see the commit that feature previously pointing to is still present, and thus we can recover safely from the rebase.

Note   While our intuition around a rebase is that we move a branch, this is not the case. New commits are made on top of the merge base, and the old commits are left without any references to them. They can thus be recovered until garbage collection occurs.

There are many diverse opinions on the case of rebasing or merging. I have a few opinions on this. First, it is key that the entire team works in a way that results in a consistent history no matter who delivers a given changeset. This most likely means everyone rebases or everyone merges. There can also be implications coming from the workflow that the team is using to develop. If, however, the workflow dictates whether you can use merges or rebases from a technical perspective, it probably needs to be looked at, and you need to reevaluate whether it is a sane way of working.

Second, if you are not working on a shared branch, you should always rebase. This leaves your history clean and bundles your commits nicely together for a concise delivery. This also makes it easier for you to manipulate your local history before you deliver, as we will cover in a later chapter. As rebasing changes the commit shas, it is considered bad practice to rebase branches that are public. However, you might be working on a public branch that are your own. It could be published to get a build from a continuous integration system, or feedback from a peer. In these cases, you should not refrain from rebasing your own, but public branch.

Tags

So far in this chapter, we have covered branches and how they are lightweight and easy to move around. There are many uses for a named reference for a commit that is more static. In Git, we have tags to supply that functionality. A tag is a reference to a commit. Commonly, tags are used to mark released versions of our source code, so we have a named reference to the source code that produced any given version of our software.

There are two types of tags, lightweight and annotated. Lightweight tags are like branches except they are static. This means that they are simply a reference to a commit with no additional information. Annotated tags are full objects in the Git object database, takes a message, and provides additional information. Annotated commits are created by adding -a, -s, or -m to the tag command. The tag command looks like this: `git tag <target>` for lightweight tags. For example, `git tag v1.6.2 a233b` will create a lightweight tag pointing at the commit with the prefix a233b.

If we omit the target, the tag will be created at HEAD.

TAGGING

In this exercise, we will go into a simple repository and add some tags and investigate them. The repository for this exercise can be found in `chapter4/tags/`.

```
$ git tag
```

First, we notice there are no tags. This is consistent with the output from the flowing log command.

```
$ git log --oneline --all
f203381 (HEAD -> feature) Add feature.txt
0a664dc (master) Add master.txt
810eb22 second commit
0cae311 Initial Commit
```

Now, we create a tag at the commit with the sha 810eb22. We use a unique prefix of the commit.

```
$ git tag v1.0 810eb
```

The tags now both show up when we list all tags, and as a reference on the log.

```
$ git tag
v1.0

$ git log --oneline --decorate --graph --all
* f203381 (HEAD -> feature) Add feature.txt
| * 0a664dc (master) Add master.txt
|/
* 810eb22 (tag: v1.0) second commit
* 0cae311 Initial Commit
```

The previous commit was made using a commit sha directly. In the following, we repeat the same flow, but rather than using a commit, we create a tag from a reference.

```
$ git tag v2.0 master

$ git tag
v1.0
v2.0

$ git log --oneline --decorate --graph --all
* f203381 (HEAD -> feature) Add feature.txt
| * 0a664dc (tag: v2.0, master) Add master.txt
```

```
| /
* 810eb22 (tag: v1.0) second commit
* 0cae311 Initial Commit
```

The previous tags are lightweight tags and are pure references. We can create full tag objects by, for instance, attaching a message to the tag.

```
$ git tag v3.0 feature -m "pre-release"
```

Having created the tag, we can see the full information on both the tag and the commit that is tagged. Contrast this with the same information on the lightweight tag.

```
$ git show v3.0
tag v3.0
Tagger: Johan Abildskov <randomsort@gmail.com>
Date:    Mon May 4 10:04:34 2020 +0200

pre-release

commit f203381f79576e69f4de2a75cd6289ea635f3543 (HEAD -> feature, tag: v3.0)
Author: Johan Abildskov <randomsort@gmail.com>
Date:    Mon May 4 10:02:12 2020 +0200

    Add feature.txt

diff --git a/feature.txt b/feature.txt
new file mode 100644
index 0000000..e69de29

$ git show v1.0
commit 810eb22a50a1bd94facd9917531295ddddd27bb7 (tag: v1.0)
Author: Johan Abildskov <randomsort@gmail.com>
Date:    Mon May 4 10:02:11 2020 +0200

    second commit

diff --git a/0.txt b/0.txt
index 303ff98..36db9be 100644
--- a/0.txt
+++ b/0.txt
@@ -1 +1,2 @@
 first file
+\n additional content
```

As we have seen in this exercise, tags can be used to mark places in our history that has some significance.

Detached HEAD

If you have had any Git experience at all before you started reading this book, it is likely that you have found yourself in a detached head situation, and it is likely that it scared you. I know because it at least took me some time before this situation did not make me feel like I did something that I should not have done.

Detached head is a completely normal situation and it is easily remedied. A detached head simply means that HEAD is pointing to a commit rather than a branch. The consequence of this is that commits created while in a detached head situation do not have any references pointing to them. This can make them disappear from git log, become garbage collected, or simply be unnecessarily difficult to get back to. The two most common ways to end up in detached HEAD are by explicitly checking out a commit or by checking out a tag. An example of this is given in Figure 4-8.

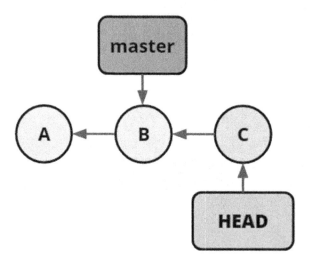

Figure 4-8. *Detached head, with a dangling commit*

If the purpose of ending up in a detached head situation is to simply look at code, to see what the state of the repository was at that point in time, there are no problems, and we can stay in the detached head state until we are ready to return to the branch we are working on. If we want to make changes, we are better off creating a branch; this can be most easily done at checkout time using the flag -b that will create a branch at the target we are checking out. This looks like `git checkout -b <branch-name> <target>`. If we want to create a branch called bugfix at the tag v1.2.7, we use the command `git checkout -b bugfix v1.2.7`.

DETACHED HEAD

In this exercise, we will put ourselves in the detached head state and recover from it. The repository for this exercise can be found in the examples as `chapter4/detached-head/`.

```
$ git log --oneline --decorate --graph --all
* adfcb1d (HEAD -> feature) Add feature.txt
| * ca3e69b (tag: v1.0, master) Add master.txt
|/
* 66d6ce7 second commit
* 66d93b9 Initial Commit
```

We check out the tag that is pointing to the same branch as the master branch.

```
$ git checkout v1.0
Note: checking out 'v1.0'.

You are in 'detached HEAD' state. You can look around, make experimental
changes and commit them, and you can discard any commits you make in this
state without impacting any branches by performing another checkout.

If you want to create a new branch to retain commits you create, you may
do so (now or later) by using -b with the checkout command again. Example:

  git checkout -b <new-branch-name>

HEAD is now at ca3e69b... Add master.txt
```

The preceding wall of text is the primary reason that a detached head feels dangerous. Note that even though there are references pointing to the commit we checked out, HEAD is not pointing to them, but directly to the commit.

```
$ git log --oneline --decorate --graph --all
* adfcb1d (feature) Add feature.txt
| * ca3e69b (HEAD, tag: v1.0, master) Add master.txt
|/
* 66d6ce7 second commit
* 66d93b9 Initial Commit

$ git checkout -b new-branch
Switched to a new branch 'new-branch'
```

Note that we have simply created and checked out a branch at HEAD. Depending on our use case, we could have checked out the master branch and continued from there.

```
$ git log --oneline --decorate --graph --all
* adfcb1d (feature) Add feature.txt
| * ca3e69b (HEAD -> new-branch, tag: v1.0, master) Add master.txt
|/
* 66d6ce7 second commit
* 66d93b9 Initial Commit
```

As can be seen from the following exercise, there is no reason to be afraid of the detached head, and it is easy to recover from.

Git Katas

In order to support the learning goals of this chapter, I recommend you go through the following katas:

- Basic-branching

- Three-way-merge

- Merge-conflict

- Merge-mergesort

- Rebase-branch

- Git-tag

- Detached-head

Summary

In this chapter, we came far about talking about branches in Git and how they work. We covered the different types of merges and contrasted merges to rebases. We walked through resolving merge conflicts. We closed off the chapter with a brief description of how we can use tags to mark interesting points in our code base. Finally, we deflated the detached head situation.

Now that we have the foundations for branches in order, we can move on to collaboration using Git.

CHAPTER 5

Collaboration in Git

As with many other things, software development is not fun until we do it together with other people. Unfortunately, most software developers are not introduced to Git in a healthy setting. Either they are experiencing Git for the setting in a classroom where the professor has understood that Git is important and that someone should be teaching it to the students, but it is simply a footnote in a much larger curriculum. Or they are introduced to workflows and collaboration in Git in some organization that are more concerned with doing things according to the described process than in a meaningful way: This chapter will hopefully get you back on track and enable you to select a Git workflow and work efficiently with colleagues.

In this chapter, we will first cover the foundations of working with a remote repository. So far, we have only concerned ourselves with local repositories. Fear not, if you have grasped branches, remotes will be a small extension of these concepts. After that, we will compare the most common workflows and discuss pros and cons of each.

Working with Remotes

Git is said to be a distributed version control system, and Git implements this distribution through the concept of remotes. Commonly, we work with a single remote in our repository, and by default, it has the name `origin`. Most development on software projects start with a clone of an existing project. This instantiates a local copy of the original repository on your computer and saves a reference to the original repository as the remote origin.

© Johan Abildskov 2020
J. Abildskov, *Practical Git*, https://doi.org/10.1007/978-1-4842-6270-2_5

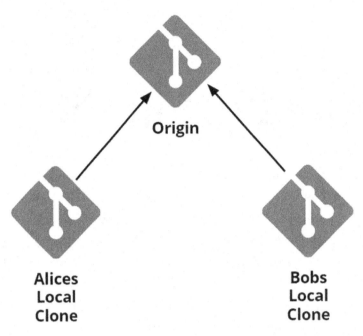

Origin

**Alices
Local
Clone**

**Bobs
Local
Clone**

Figure 5-1. *Git repository managed centrally, but cloned locally. Alice and Bob can work asynchronously and either coordinate work at the origin or between each other*

In client/server-based version control systems, all commands and actions go through the server. This means that we can do things like lock files, so only one user at a time can modify it. In Git, it is not so. We work asynchronously and then at the user's leisure synchronize our work. Most commonly, this is done through a common repository manager such as GitHub.

Most of the tasks in collaboration flow around how we manage branches, but other than that, we work with clone, fetch, push, and pull. With these four commands, 98% of your day-to-day collaboration work will be covered.

Note   Collaboration typically takes place on a managed server or cloud solution such as GitHub, GitLab, or Bitbucket. For the purpose of creating self-contained exercises, we are not using a repository manager. We are modeling the workflows using local repositories. The last exercise in this chapter should you choose to complete it requires an account on GitHub and will show off a repository manager.

Cloning

There are two scenarios for starting work on a project. First, it can be a new project. We covered that scenario a long time ago, using git init. Second and perhaps more common, we are going to contribute to an existing code base, open source or proprietary. When starting on an existing code base, the first thing that we do is to clone the repository in order to get a local instance on our machine. We do this with the command git clone <url> <path>, for example, git clone https://github.com/randomsort/practical-git/ git-exercises. This will initialize a local repository on disk, download the entire repository from the remote, check out the default branch into the workspace, and create a pointer to the remote repository named origin. The default branch in most cases is the master branch. If we omit the path parameter, Git will use the repository name instead. In the preceding example, it would be in a folder called practical-git if we omit the path.

CLONING A REPOSITORY

In this exercise, we will clone a public repository from GitHub and look at what we get on our disk. This exercise can be done from anywhere, so is not dependent on the exercise source bundled with this book.

First, we clone the repository https://github.com/randomsort/practical-git-students.

Git tells us a lot about what is going on during the clone, but it is basically uninteresting facts on performance. Consider it a geeky progress bar.

```
$ git clone https://github.com/randomsort/practical-git-students git-exercises
Cloning into 'git-exercises'...
remote: Enumerating objects: 7, done.
remote: Counting objects: 100% (7/7), done.
remote: Compressing objects: 100% (6/6), done.
remote: Total 7 (delta 1), reused 2 (delta 0), pack-reused 0
Unpacking objects: 100% (7/7), done.

$ cd git-exercises/

$ git status
On branch master
Your branch is up-to-date with 'origin/master'.
```

```
nothing to commit, working tree clean
```

```
$ ls
README.md  the-practical-git.md
```

Navigate to the repository and use git status and ls to let us know what we downloaded. We can see that there are a few files, that we have a clean workspace, and that the master branch is up to date with the remote. This is as expected as we have done no work in the repository.

```
$ git log --oneline -n 5
f18e7bc (HEAD -> master, origin/master, origin/HEAD) Merge pull request #1
from the-practical-git/master
1135048 Add the Practical Git Bio
ce866b9 Initial commit
```

We use git log to see the history. This will likely look different for you, as more pull requests enter the repository on a frequent basis. Here, we can both see the local branches and those from the remote. The remote branches are prefixed with origin/.

```
$ git remote show origin
```

We use the command git remote show origin to see some details about our remote.

```
* remote origin
  Fetch URL: https://github.com/randomsort/practical-git-students
  Push  URL: https://github.com/randomsort/practical-git-students
  HEAD branch: master
  Remote branch:
    master tracked
```

This section shows the basic information about the repository's remote. Usually, fetch and push point to the same repository, but if you have a highly distributed setup, there is the possibility of having different read and write servers.

```
  Local branch configured for 'git pull':
    master merges with remote master
  Local ref configured for 'git push':
    master pushes to master (up to date)
```

```
$ git branch
* master
```

```
$ git branch --remote
  origin/HEAD -> origin/master
  origin/master
```

This exercise showed you how you could clone a repository and see the origin.

Synchronizing with Remote

Now that our local repository is established, we are set up to do some work. The common workflow in Git is to do some work locally and then synchronize that work with the remote. Delivering our work to the remote is called pushing. When there is work available on the remote that we do not have locally, we can get that work using pull or fetch. There are a few types of differences that can occur between a local remote. They can either be about objects or references. For the purpose of this chapter, commits are the only type of objects we concern ourselves with. When we synchronize objects, it is always an additive operation. We always deliver more objects or download more objects. We can never delete or modify objects either locally or remotely. This makes object operations safe, as we never lose an object, bar garbage collection. Secondly, we can need to synchronize references, that is, branches and tags. They can either disagree on what they point to or whether they should exist at all.

These divergences are reconciled using branching methods and the methods for interacting with the remote: push, fetch, and pull. Pull is a shorthand for a fetch and a merge. Push is the least interesting of the commands. We send the references and objects that we have to the remote – and if the remote is unable to do a fast-forward merge on the references, then it will reject the change.

When we fetch, we get all the objects from the remote that we are missing. Then, we get the references from the remote. They are name spaced such that references from the remote named origin are prefixed with origin/; thus, the master branch on the origin is called origin/master when we look at it from our local repository. Thus, the flow for getting the changes from the master on origin is as follows:

- **Fetch**: To get objects and references from remote

- **Merge**: To get the changes from the remote onto our local master branch

This can be seen in Figure 5-2.

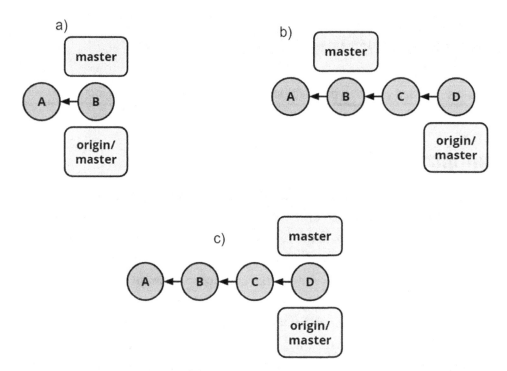

Figure 5-2. *(a) Repository before fetching. (b) Repository after fetching. (c) Repository after merging*

When we push and get our changes rejected, we go through a fetch/merge loop and will then be able to deliver our changes.

Note   We can see the origin/ namespace as our cache of how the remote repository looks. This is not automatically synchronized by Git, so we need to do the fetch to update our cache. Thus, when we run Git status, the output is based on our cache, rather than what is on the remote, and this might yield to unexpected results.

We will cover how this plays out in the next exercise based on the simplified workflow. Now that we have investigated the moving parts of working with a remote, we can see the different ways of working and how we can work within them.

Simplified Workflow

You might have come across the term simplified workflow, master based or centralized workflow. This workflow is known by many names and is default workflow unless you configured your repository manager differently. The defining characteristic of this workflow is that all collaboration happens directly on the master. This means that while you may have local branches to isolate your work, when you are done, you push to master. This workflow is how I work with my toy projects, note repositories, and similar things. The good thing is there is little overhead and almost no process. This makes it an efficient workflow that is easy to understand, that is, if we stay on the happy path. The bad thing is that we can have race conditions with our colleagues, and we have no workflow tools that help keep the quality of the source on our master branch high.

There are basically two scenarios that we need to cover in a master-based workflow. First, there is the happy scenario where no work has been done in master while we have been working locally. This case is boring, as this works, and becomes a fast-forward merge on the remote. This scenario can be seen in Figure 5-3.

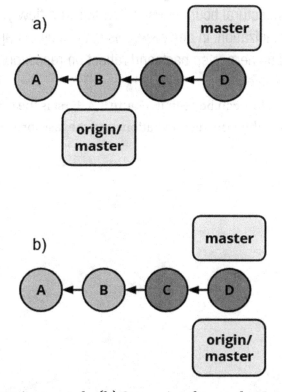

Figure 5-3. *(a) Scenario prepush. (b) Scenario after push. Note that before the push, C and D are not available on the remote*

Then, there is the race condition scenario where a colleague has delivered work to the master branch while we were working locally. This is a much interesting scenario, as it takes some measure of effort to resolve. The technical detail is that repository managers only allow you to push fast-forward merges. Any other types of merges must be reconciled locally. This means that the scenario with competing deliveries looks like this:

- Clone or fetch from origin.

- Do work locally and commit.

- Push, and be rejected from remote.

- Fetch newest changes and merge them into your local master branch.

- Push master to origin, as it is now a fast-forward merge.

Note   It is entirely possible that this can happen repeatedly thus locking out developers from delivering their changes. This either means that the repository spans too many architectural boundaries or that the workflow you are using is not scaling with your organization. In any case, this is unlikely to happen for normal usage, so if you end up here, step back and reflect on repository architecture.

The preceding workflow can be seen in Figure 5-4. First is the scenario where local changes will be rejected, then the reconciliation, and the fast-forward merge on the remote.

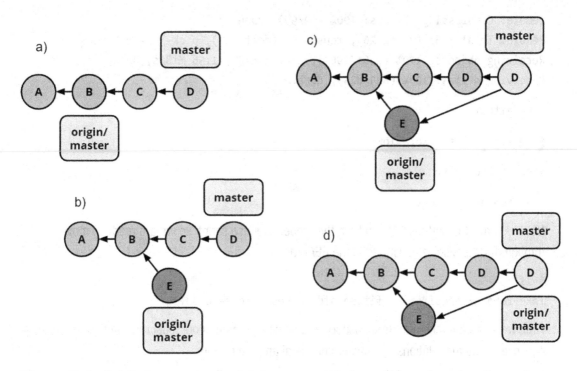

Figure 5-4. *(a) Before we push, this is our world view; (b) as there has been done work on master on the remote (commit E), push will be rejected. After fetch, this is how it looks (c). We reconcile the differences with a merge, and the result can be pushed which leads to (d) status after push*

In the following, we will do an exercise that simulates interacting with a remote repository on the master branch. As this is a more complex exercise than the previous exercises, I am going to run through the master-workflow kata in this exercise. The kata is available in the git-kata repository.

MASTER-BASED WORKFLOW

In this exercise, we are going to go through the entire master-workflow kata and experience both the happy path and the path with a race condition.

```
$ git clone https://github.com/praqma-training/gitkatas
Cloning into 'gitkatas'...
remote: Enumerating objects: 111, done.
remote: Counting objects: 100% (111/111), done.
```

```
remote: Compressing objects: 100% (99/99), done.
remote: Total 1961 (delta 26), reused 35 (delta 10), pack-reused 1850
Receiving objects: 100% (1961/1961), 528.24 KiB | 1.56 MiB/s, done.
Resolving deltas: 100% (825/825), done.

$ cd gitkatas/

$ cd master-based-workflow/

$ source setup.sh

--- Truncated Output ---
```

Now, we have fetched the kata and run the proper exercise script, so we are ready to move through the exercise as described in the README.

```
$ ls
fake-remote-repository/  fitzgerald-pushes-before-we-do.sh*
```

First, we clone the fake remote repository and make a commit in our local repository. Then, we can investigate the relationship between our local and the remote.

```
$ git clone fake-remote-repository/ local-repo
Cloning into 'local-repo'...
done.

$ cd local-repo/

$ echo "line of text" >> README.md

$ git status
On branch master
Your branch is up-to-date with 'origin/master'.

Changes not staged for commit:
  (use "git add <file>..." to update what will be committed)
  (use "git checkout -- <file>..." to discard changes in working directory)

        modified:   README.md

no changes added to commit (use "git add" and/or "git commit -a")
```

We note that since we have not created any commits, we are still up to date with the remote master, also designated origin/master.

```
$ git add .
```

```
$ git commit -m "Added content to the README"
[master 9eea570] Added content to the README
 1 file changed, 1 insertion(+)
```

```
$ git status
On branch master
Your branch is ahead of 'origin/master' by 1 commit.
  (use "git push" to publish your local commits)
```

```
nothing to commit, working tree clean
```

As we have created a single commit, and no work has been done on the remote, we are up to date.

```
$ git push
Counting objects: 3, done.
Writing objects: 100% (3/3), 279 bytes | 279.00 KiB/s, done.
Total 3 (delta 0), reused 0 (delta 0)
To C:/Users/rando/repos/randomsort/gitkatas/master-based-workflow/exercise/
fake-remote-repository/
   054c055..9eea570  master -> master
```

We can now deliver a change to the remote and move on to the nonhappy path scenario.

```
$ echo "Another line of text" >> README.md
```

```
$ git add README.md
```

```
$ git commit -m "Update README"
[master d144b48] Update README
 1 file changed, 1 insertion(+)
```

Now, after we have updated the README and made another commit, we run a script to simulate our colleague delivering work.

```
$ ../fitzgerald-pushes-before-we-do.sh
 --- Output truncated ---
```

```
$ git push
To C:/Users/rando/repos/randomsort/gitkatas/master-based-workflow/exercise/
fake-remote-repository/
 ! [rejected]        master -> master (fetch first)
error: failed to push some refs to 'C:/Users/rando/repos/randomsort/gitkatas/
master-based-workflow/exercise/fake-remote-repository/'
hint: Updates were rejected because the remote contains work that you do
```

93

```
hint: not have locally. This is usually caused by another repository pushing
hint: to the same ref. You may want to first integrate the remote changes
hint: (e.g., 'git pull ...') before pushing again.
hint: See the 'Note about fast-forwards' in 'git push --help' for details.
```

Now when we try to push, we get rejected by the remote. If we read the error output, we can see that our push is rejected because the remote contains work that we do not. However, when we run git status, we are told we are up to date.

```
$ git status
On branch master
Your branch is ahead of 'origin/master' by 1 commit.
  (use "git push" to publish your local commits)

nothing to commit, working tree clean
```

This is because we have a local cache of the remote state and that is not updated when we push, but rather during the fetch.

```
$ git fetch
remote: Counting objects: 3, done.
remote: Compressing objects: 100% (2/2), done.
remote: Total 3 (delta 0), reused 0 (delta 0)
Unpacking objects: 100% (3/3), done.
From C:/Users/rando/repos/randomsort/gitkatas/master-based-workflow/exercise/
fake-remote-repository
   9eea570..96a3f9c  master     -> origin/master
```

```
$ git status
On branch master
Your branch and 'origin/master' have diverged,
and have 1 and 1 different commits each, respectively.
  (use "git pull" to merge the remote branch into yours)

nothing to commit, working tree clean
```

After the fetch, status tells us that we have diverged from origin/master. This is the scenario shown in Figure 5-4(b).

```
$ git log --all --graph --decorate --oneline
* 96a3f9c (origin/master, origin/HEAD) Fitz made this
| * d144b48 (HEAD -> master) Update README
|/
* 9eea570 Added content to the README
* 054c055 Add README.md

$ git merge origin/master -m "merge"
Merge made by the 'recursive' strategy.
 fitz-was-here.md | 0
 1 file changed, 0 insertions(+), 0 deletions(-)
 create mode 100644 fitz-was-here.md
$ git merge origin/master

$ git status
On branch master
Your branch is ahead of 'origin/master' by 2 commits.
  (use "git push" to publish your local commits)

nothing to commit, working tree clean
```

After we have merged, we are in the state as shown in Figure 5-4(c). We are two commits ahead, the commit we had locally and the merge commit.

```
$ git log --all --oneline --decorate --graph
*   a73deeb (HEAD -> master) Merge remote-tracking branch 'origin/master'
|\
| * 96a3f9c (origin/master, origin/HEAD) Fitz made this
* | d144b48 Update README
|/
* 9eea570 Added content to the README
* 054c055 Add README.md
```

We can now push as we have established the conditions for a fast-forward merge from origin/master to master.

```
$ git push
Counting objects: 5, done.
Delta compression using up to 4 threads.
Compressing objects: 100% (3/3), done.
Writing objects: 100% (5/5), 582 bytes | 582.00 KiB/s, done.
Total 5 (delta 0), reused 0 (delta 0)
```

```
To C:/Users/rando/repos/randomsort/gitkatas/master-based-workflow/exercise/
fake-remote-repository/
   96a3f9c..a73deeb  master -> master

$ git status
On branch master
Your branch is up-to-date with 'origin/master'.

nothing to commit, working tree clean
```

As we have seen in this exercise, nothing tremendously exciting is happening, and it is simple to reconcile the race condition in this simple scenario. If you encounter many merge conflicts, this is a sign that you should investigate a different way of working.

The master-based workflow is not bad for simple projects, and the low amount of overhead and process is attractive for many. If you are just starting out, this is a good workflow to get your bearings. If you continuously pay attention to whether the lack of process is hurting your productivity, you should be good.

Fork-Based Workflows

Fork-based workflows are commonly used in open source software, where the trust model is a bit different than inside an organization. While open source means that everyone can contribute, it does not mean that all changes will get into the projects. The fork-based workflow helps enable this way of working.

In fork-based workflows, we have multiple remote repositories. One of which is the original and contains the ultimate truth of the project. Let us say that I want to contribute to a major open source project such as Kubernetes. I can't simply clone the repository and push back any changes I would like. First, there is the issue of the quality of my delivery, what if I am horribly incompetent and my work should be kept out? Second, there is also the vision of the product. If there are no clear vision and guidelines to what features the project is interested in supporting, it will become an unmaintainable and unusable mess over time. Thus, even if my work is good, the project might not be interested in integrating it. And lastly, the two previous points were even assuming that my intentions were benign. If we do not have guard rails or some sort of access control, all open source projects would be instantly compromised by bad third parties. There have been situations where evil actors have injected vulnerabilities in high-profile open source projects, thus compromising all those that depended on that code.

The solution to this is that we create a so-called fork of the original project, on our own namespace. This gives us full access to our fork. We can then make our changes and submit those back to the original project using a mechanic commonly called pull requests. This can be seen in Figure 5-5.

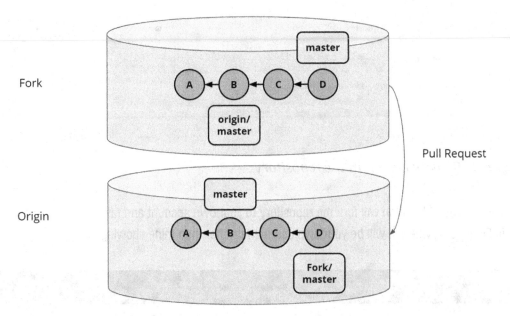

Figure 5-5. *A pull request from a fork to the original repository. Commonly, the owner of the fork has no access rights to the original repository*

Note   It is called pull requests because you make a second remote available and request the maintainers to pull your changes into their repository.

FORK-BASED WORKFLOW

This exercise is a bit different in that it will require a GitHub account, and it will be based more on screenshots than on command-line interface.

If, however, you complete this exercise, you will have contributed to a public repository on GitHub.

This exercise assumes that you have a GitHub account and that you are logged in.

First, we are going to locate the repository that we are going to contribute to and create a fork of that.

To do so, open `https://github.com/randomsort/practical-git-students` in your browser and locate the fork button as seen in Figure 5-6.

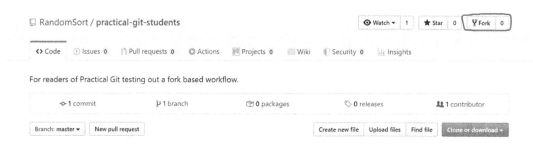

Figure 5-6. *Fork button in the repository*

Clicking the fork button will fork the repository to your own account and take you to this page in Figure 5-7, where it will be your own username rather than mine showing up.

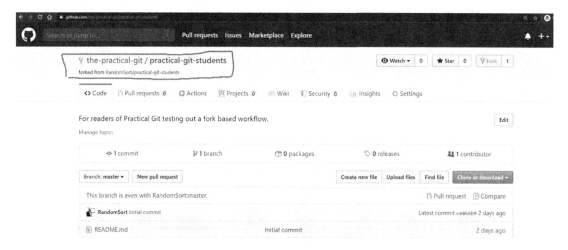

Figure 5-7. *Forking the repository to your account*

We can note that it is explicit from where we have forked the repository.

Now that we have our own fork, or working copy, we can clone this link, either through the clone button or the command line.

I will clone through the command line. I will not cover how to set up credentials or anything here.

```
$ git clone https://github.com/the-practical-git/practical-git-students
Cloning into 'practical-git-students'...
remote: Enumerating objects: 3, done.
remote: Counting objects: 100% (3/3), done.
remote: Compressing objects: 100% (2/2), done.
remote: Total 3 (delta 0), reused 0 (delta 0), pack-reused 0
Unpacking objects: 100% (3/3), done.
```

I will now go into the folder and create a file with my bio in it.

```
$ cd practical-git-students/

$ touch the-practical-git.md

$ vim the-practical-git.md

$ git add .

$ git commit -m "Add the Practical Git Bio"
[master 1135048] Add the Practical Git Bio
 1 file changed, 11 insertions(+)
 create mode 100644 the-practical-git.md

$ git push
Username for 'https://github.com': the-practical-git
Counting objects: 3, done.
Delta compression using up to 4 threads.
Compressing objects: 100% (3/3), done.
Writing objects: 100% (3/3), 493 bytes | 493.00 KiB/s, done.
Total 3 (delta 0), reused 0 (delta 0)
To https://github.com/the-practical-git/practical-git-students
   ce866b9..1135048  master -> master
```

Note that if you are following along with the exercise, you should choose your own name or username as the filename, and you should use your own username for authenticating for GitHub. Depending on how your local Git installation is configured you may be prompted for credentials, or it might just work.

Now, we can go back to our fork and see that the changes we made showed up in the GitHub interface. For me, I go to `https://github.com/the-practical-git/practical-git-students`, but you will have to substitute with your own username.

We can see in Figure 5-8 that we now have a commit that is not present in the original repository. This is what we would like to contribute back! So we click the Pull request link to the right.

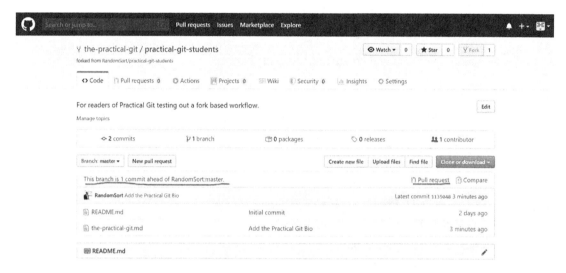

Figure 5-8. *Commit in your repository – click Pull request*

This takes us to Figure 5-9 where we can see the changeset and what branches we are using. In this case, we will contribute back to the master branch in the original repository, what is on our master branch in our fork. So we click the Create pull request button.

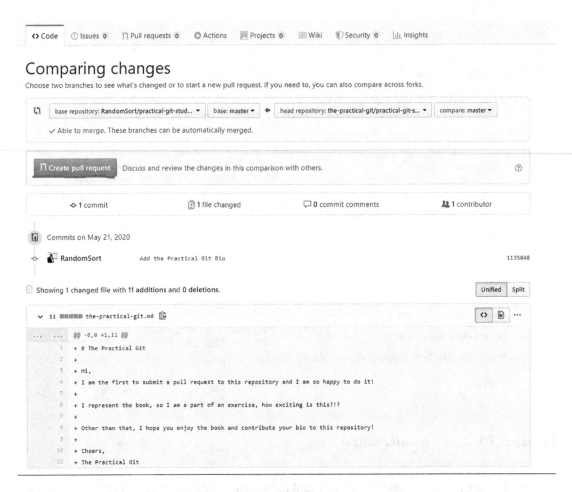

Figure 5-9. *Seeing the changeset. Create pull request*

This takes us to Figure 5-10 where we can add a bit more information to the pull request. Commonly, we will describe the changeset, or the reason for the change. This is our communication toward the maintainers of the repository. In this case, our changeset is trivial, so we only add a brief description before clicking Create pull request.

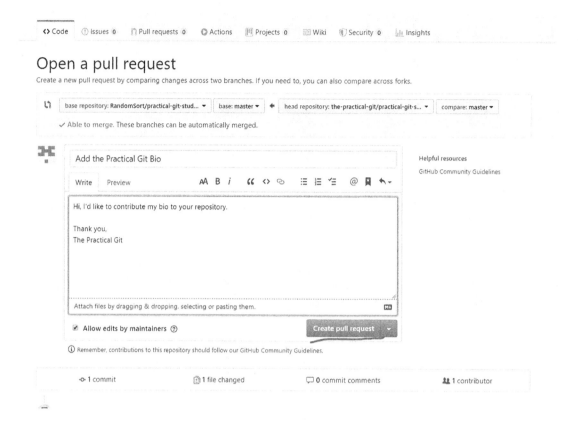

Figure 5-10. *Open a pull request*

In many scenarios, there will be a bit back and forth between the contributors and the maintainers to make sure that the pull request adheres to their coding guidelines, has the documentation and tests they need, and so on. In this case, I will accept your pull request, if you keep the language clean and kind, and do not cover political or religious issue. I would love for you to say Hi, though!

Now that you have created the pull request, your work is done, unless there are any requests by the maintainers for reworks. From the maintainer side, we can now go and find the pull request in the Pull requests tab, as seen in Figure 5-11.

Figure 5-11. *Pull requests tab*

We click the pull request to see what is being contributed, and here we can comment and interact with the contributor (Figure 5-12).

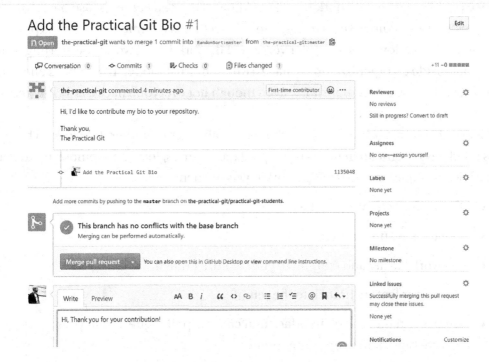

Figure 5-12. *Interact with pull request contributor*

As the maintainer, I can click the Merge pull request and accept your changes. If you have been following along with this exercise, I am looking forward to merging in your commits!

Note that while this exercise was performed in GitHub, all the big repository managers support fork-based workflows.

This has been an exercise into fork-based workflows, commonly used in open source setups. I know some open source projects who have their source in Git have different email-based systems, but that is so arcane and not used a lot that we will not go into details on that. In the next section, we will present the more commonly used workflow inside of organizations.

Pull Request–Based Workflows

While we could argue that the fork-based workflow described earlier is also based on pull requests, the workflow we go through in this section is commonly known as pull request–based workflow. It is a simpler version of the fork-based workflow, starting from the fact that inside an organization we have a different trust model. Everyone is allowed to contribute directly to the repository, even though not everyone necessarily has access rights to merge to the master branch.

The way this works is by using branches as the abstraction rather than forks. This causes much less overhead in terms of keeping repositories, local and remote, up to date. The workflow in a pull request–based workflow is as such:

- Clone or fetch the repository.
- Create a feature branch.
- Do work locally and commit to your feature branch.
- Push your feature branch to the remote.
- Go to the remotes web interface and create a pull request from your feature branch to your master branch.
- Those that have access rights merge or request changes.

The pull request–based workflow is simple, understandable, and does not have a lot of overhead. However, pull requests lend themselves to a few antipatterns that we will cover here. First, depending on your way of working, pull requests might be a manual gate, requiring reviews and manual approval. This can lead to handoffs and delayed feedback loops; this reduces productivity and morale and leads to lower-quality software.

Second, pull requests tend to be created late in the development process, when we are ready to deliver. To great effect, they can be created at the start of the process as a work in progress branch. This will create traceability and add the ability for early feedback on work, and collaboration, which increases productivity.

Third, when many pull requests target the same master branch, this can also lead to issues in synchronizing and maintaining the pull request, while those that are in front in the queue get processed. This can also lead to broken builds on the master due to tests being run on another state that ends up being merged.

Again, if this is something that you encounter, you have outgrown this way of working, or your repository architecture.

Git Flow

I have had a long inner discussion on whether to cover the Git Flow or not. It is a workflow that I have seen many organizations adapt, and none succeed with. It is described by nvie in his blog post at https://nvie.com/posts/a-successful-git-branching-model/ as "a successful git branching model." While I am certain that some organizations have had good fortune with this workflow, but Git, the tools that surround it, and our ways of working have outgrown it. Thus, Git Flow is, for most uses, an antipattern. The problems that we try to solve by introducing the abstractions and the "develop" branch often end up with doing the exact opposite. We end up with long merge queues, complex workflows, and integration hell in multiple directions. So, I do really recommend against it.

The scenario I can imagine where Git Flow is useful is if you have a completely dysfunctional way of working and you need a temporary transition flow in order to get to a sane place. This can help with the organizational resistance, tooling, and upskilling as required.

Git Katas

To support this chapter's learning goals, I recommend that you go through your master-workflow kata of the previous exercise. After that, if you have not already covered the exercise doing a pull request on GitHub, I suggest you backtrack to that and make the pull request now. I look forward to saying Hi and hearing from you!

Summary

In this chapter, we covered a few basic Git workflows and showed how you can collaborate using Git. Hopefully, you now feel more confident that you can be a valuable contributor in a software organization. It is important to me that you take charge of your workflow and do not let the workflow dictate how you work, but rather let the way you work dictate your workflow. If there is a mismatch between the desired way of working and the implemented Git workflow, you will live in pain and frustration.

I recommend that you consider the following questions on a routine basis:

- Is my workflow introducing manual gates or handoffs?

- Is my workflow making it easy to deliver changes?

- Do I feel confident in our workflow?

- Does the workflow introduce unnecessary bureaucracy?

- What are the common mistakes that our developers make? Can we do something to minimize either the impact or frequency of these?

If we keep asking these questions and accept that our workflow is not a dead static thing, but rather something that lives and evolves together with our software, we will end up in a good place.

CHAPTER 6

Manipulating History

It may seem very counterintuitive that I put a full chapter into manipulating history. Version control is at its core about traceability, reproducibility, and immutability. But Git lets you manipulate the history. For any public history, published to colleagues or available on the Internet, we must tread very carefully and use with care and responsibility the powers this chapter bestows us. But for local history, before we'd publish it can bring tremendous value to sculpt the version history to fit the logical units.

In this chapter, we will first cover undo a change that is present in our history with revert. This allows us to safely undo previous work while maintaining full traceability and immutability.

Next, we are going to cover reset which is the big red button for undoing large chunks of our history, and not just removing changes from our workspace but also removing them from our history. It also does less impactful stuff and is my favorite tool for juggling branches locally.

Last, we cover the interactive rebase which allows us to combine, split, delete, and reorder commits in our history. This is an extremely powerful tool, but can feel a bit scary, and again should be kept a long distance from public history. In terms of delivering the best possible history to colleagues or your future self, no tool is better.

Reverting Commits

There are many scenarios where we need to undo some change in our history. If we are lucky, it is the most recent change, but likely it is not. These changes that we'd like to remove from our applications can be bugs introduced, features no longer used, or simply some clutter that we would like to remove. In this scenario, where we have a specific commit that introduces a change that we would like to remove, we can use git revert. The logic of git revert is that it creates a commit that is the reverse changeset of the commit that we want to revert. This can be seen in Figure 6-1.

© Johan Abildskov 2020
J. Abildskov, *Practical Git*, https://doi.org/10.1007/978-1-4842-6270-2_6

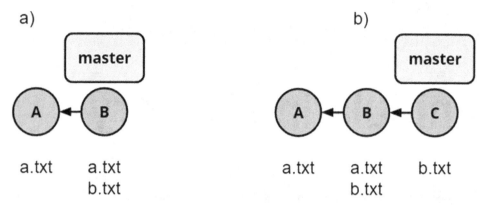

Figure 6-1. *(a) Two commits adding a file each. (b) History after running the command git revert a*

In this scenario, we are not actively manipulating history, we are rather using Git as a shortcut to revert a change. Without Git, we would be forced to manually try and figure out how to undo the given changes and then create that commit ourselves.

This also means that we are not doing anything that can compromise the traceability established through Git. As such, it is safe from an auditing perspective to use revert on public history. Whether you are breaking any functionality that you did not intend is beyond the scope of Git. Always run your tests!

REVERT EXERCISE

In this exercise, we will go through reverting a commit. The repository for this exercise can be found in the source code in Chapter 6 in the folder `revert/`.

```
$ ls
a.txt  b.txt
```

```
$ git log --oneline
5be4a3d (HEAD -> master) Add File B
c8482f6 Add File A
```

We see a simple history and we want to undo the changes introduced in commit `c8482` with the message "Add File A".

First, we use `git show` to see what changeset the commit represents.

```
$ git show c8482
```

```
commit c8482f67747fd8dcb6ced373d89ce3e8dc7d7754
Author: Johan Abildskov <randomsort@gmail.com>
Date:    Sun Jun 14 16:05:10 2020 +0200

    Add File A
```

diff --git a/a.txt b/a.txt
new file mode 100644
index 0000000..4ef30bb
--- /dev/null
+++ b/a.txt
```
@@ -0,0 +1 @@
+file a
```

Besides the ordinary commit information, we also see the diff. Here, we can see that the file a.txt was created. This is the basis for what we will revert.

```
$ git revert c8482
Removing a.txt
hint: Waiting for your editor to close the file...
[master 26dc609] Revert "Add File A"
 1 file changed, 1 deletion(-)
 delete mode 100644 a.txt
```

When we target the commit to revert, we get the usual commit message prompt. It is prefilled with a sane message, so we can save the file and have Git create the commit.

```
$ git log --oneline
26dc609 (HEAD -> master) Revert "Add File A"
5be4a3d Add File B
c8482f6 Add File A
```

We observe that Git has created a new commit, so let us see what it contains.

```
$ git show 26dc
commit 26dc6094fbbd6293bb2a69f354d78008194ea6c3 (HEAD -> master)
Author: Johan Abildskov <randomsort@gmail.com>
Date:    Sun Jun 14 16:05:53 2020 +0200

    Revert "Add File A"

    This reverts commit c8482f67747fd8dcb6ced373d89ce3e8dc7d7754.
```

```
diff --git a/a.txt b/a.txt
deleted file mode 100644
index 4ef30bb..0000000
--- a/a.txt
+++ /dev/null
@@ -1 +0,0 @@
-file a
```

Here, we get the exact opposite of the commit we reverted, namely, that the file is no longer present. We get a bit more elaboration in the body of the commit message as the trace to the original commit is maintained.

```
$ ls
b.txt
```

As expected, we now only have b.txt in our workspace. As has been shown in this exercise, reverting commits can be a safe way to undo a change introduced at an arbitrary point in history.

Reverting commits can be done easily and safely if you as a developer take care of the semantics of the changes you are juggling. It will likely be safer than trying to revert changes manually, without tool assistance. Git tooling like revert and others are another good reason to make your commits atomic and self-contained.

Reset

Reset is one of my favorite Git commands, not only because of its powerful functionality but also because it is one of the commands that allow us to uncover the most knowledge on how Git works and how our intuition might be in conflict with this.

Git is overall very conservative with taking actions that might cause you to lose your work unexpectedly. Git reset, in its hard mode, is one of the ways that Git will throw away unsaved work without warning. It does require an active choice by the user, so this is not too bad in itself. Unfortunately, reset is also one of the commands that have a horrible user experience. I hope to guide you through the command and combined with the exercise and doing the katas that you will feel confident introducing the reset command in your everyday coding life.

Git reset has three modes: soft, mixed, and hard. We will go through them in turn and end up with an exercise covering all three.

Soft Reset

In the soft mode, `git reset --soft <ref>`, we are only manipulating HEAD. That is, the reference currently checked out will be changed to the target given as an argument. In other words, the soft reset can be used to move a branch pointer.

This can be useful if, for instance, you forgot to create your feature branch before you started your work and thus have created your commits on master. Then, you could make it look like you did the right thing all along by first creating your feature branch at `master` and then resetting `--soft master` to `origin/master`.

As the soft reset leaves both the working directory and the stage alone, it is a completely safe operation. Figure 6-2 shows updating the branch pointer.

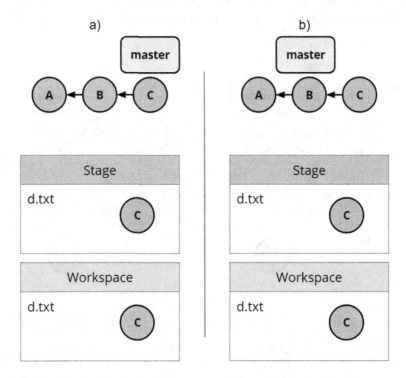

Figure 6-2. *(b) Is the result from starting in (a) and running git reset --soft B*

The soft reset can be used to squash a series of commits together into a single commit. It is done by resetting to the point from which your work started and then creating a commit. The squash works because all your work, represented by the newest commit, will then be in the stage that you can commit into a single commit. This is not a typical scenario and is usually better solved by the interactive rebase that we will cover later in this chapter.

Mixed Reset

The mixed reset is the default behavior when you do not pass a mode to git reset. Mixed reset, besides updating HEAD as soft does, also updates the stage to the targeted place. When we do not pass any ref to reset, HEAD is the default behavior. This leads to the confusing situation that the most common use case for reset --mixed is unstaging files. That is if you have at some point used git add to stage a path, and you no longer want that path to be staged, you can use the command git reset <path>. The logic is that you overwrite the stage with what is in the commit pointed to by the ref, which is HEAD by default. It took me some time to wrap my head around the fact that to remove something from the stage, you have to put something else there.

Figure 6-3 shows this scenario. In it, we also show the stage, which unless something has been added to it will be equivalent to the content in HEAD.

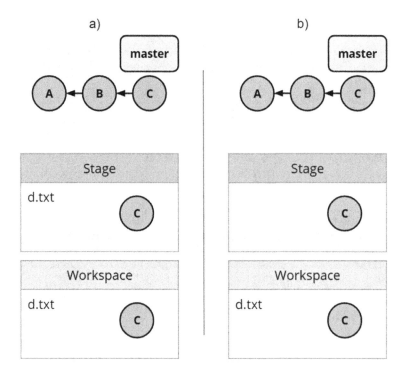

Figure 6-3. *Showing that git reset d.txt changes the stage, but not the workspace*

Based on the earlier texts, a reasonable question would be, what would happen if we reset mixed to B, for instance? In this case, we would put B and only B into the stage and update HEAD.

Hard Reset

As mentioned before, the hard reset is one of the only dangerous commands in Git – at least from the perspective of how likely Git is to throw away your work without giving you a warning. The mixed reset updates HEAD and the stage, with the content of the target ref. Hard reset updates HEAD, the stage, and the working directory. This means that not only unsaved work but also work that is not a part of a commit will be lost. This is one of the few ways that Git can overwrite your work in an unrecoverable way. So, proceed with caution. The hard reset is part of my daily Git routine, and it could also be part of yours; just make sure that you do it deliberately. Figure 6-4 shows how the hard reset changes both the stage, workspace, and HEAD.

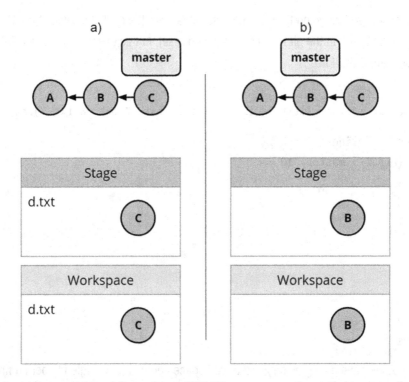

Figure 6-4. *git reset --hard B updates HEAD, stage, and workspace to the content of B*

While the hard reset is considered off limits by some, it is part of my day-to-day workflow. If we are disciplined around making commits often and take care in running git status before we do a hard reset, we have a powerful and simple tool at our disposal. I have many times seen developers accidentally messing up their local histories with pulls when they did not mean to, or by having contaminated their master branch. The way I do this personally is by avoiding pull in all but the simplest cases. Most often, I will use `git fetch` to update my local cache and then use `git reset --hard origin/master` to start from the most up-to-date scratch. When I have made certain to keep my work on isolated branches, this is a safe command to run.

RESET EXERCISE

In this exercise, I will be going through the reset kata from the git-katas repository. This exercise can be found in the git katas and is called reset. In this exercise, we use HEAD~1 to refer to the parent of HEAD.

```
$ ls
1.txt  10.txt  2.txt  3.txt  4.txt  5.txt  6.txt  7.txt  8.txt  9.txt

$ git log --oneline
6742e05 (HEAD -> master) 10
76ac07a 9
c3e33b7 8
da46ca2 7
1d9b4de 6
21a5ff1 5
a7e2065 4
065ebe8 3
df9cfa3 2
89514e1 1
```

We note that we have a long history and a workspace containing a single file per commit. We do not investigate, but it is safe to assume that each file is added in the corresponding commit.

```
$ git reset --soft HEAD~1

$ git log --oneline
76ac07a (HEAD -> master) 9
```

```
c3e33b7 8
da46ca2 7
1d9b4de 6
21a5ff1 5
a7e2065 4
065ebe8 3
df9cfa3 2
89514e1 1
```

We note that the `master` branch is now pointing to the commit 9 rather than 10.

Investigating the workspace and `git status` shows us that indeed stage and workspace still have the content from 10.

```
$ ls
1.txt   10.txt   2.txt   3.txt   4.txt   5.txt   6.txt   7.txt   8.txt   9.txt

$ git status
On branch master
Changes to be committed:
  (use "git restore --staged <file>..." to unstage)
        new file:    10.txt
```

Now, we can `reset --mixed` and the log shows us that we have again moved on.

```
$ git reset --mixed HEAD~1

$ git log --oneline
c3e33b7 (HEAD -> master) 8
da46ca2 7
1d9b4de 6
21a5ff1 5
a7e2065 4
065ebe8 3
df9cfa3 2
89514e1 1

$ ls
1.txt   10.txt   2.txt   3.txt   4.txt   5.txt   6.txt   7.txt   8.txt   9.txt

$ git status
On branch master
```

```
Untracked files:
  (use "git add <file>..." to include in what will be committed)
        10.txt
        9.txt
```

```
nothing added to commit but untracked files present (use "git add" to track)
```

Looking in the workspace and checking the status shows us that we still have not changed our workspace, but now 9.txt and 10.txt are untracked, as the stage matches the content in 8.

```
$ git reset --hard HEAD~1
HEAD is now at da46ca2 7
```

```
$ git log --oneline
da46ca2 (HEAD -> master) 7
1d9b4de 6
21a5ff1 5
a7e2065 4
065ebe8 3
df9cfa3 2
89514e1 1
```

Resetting hard continues the trend of updating HEAD. But now, we are resetting hard, so we expect our workspace to change. Before moving on, I suggest you spend a few moments pondering how you expect the workspace to look.

```
$ ls
1.txt  10.txt  2.txt  3.txt  4.txt  5.txt  6.txt  7.txt  9.txt
```

A peculiar thing is happening here. 8.txt is missing, but 9.txt and 10.txt are still present in the workspace. This happens because 9 and 10 are untracked because of our previous actions. As such, Git does not care about them at this time, and they will be left in the workspace.

```
$ git status
On branch master
Untracked files:
  (use "git add <file>..." to include in what will be committed)
        10.txt
        9.txt
```

```
nothing added to commit but untracked files present (use "git add" to track)
```

So now we have seen the three different modes of the git reset command. It can be daunting and this kata is my favorite one because it encapsulates a lot of learning. This is why I really recommend you go through this kata a few times, until you have built your reset intuition and can wield git reset --hard like a ninja.

In this section, we have been using reset in all its modes for different purposes. One important thing to remember is that no matter what, if you put your data in a commit, you can restore it, even after a hard reset. I hope this section has shown you the power that this safety can give you.

Interactive Rebase

Some of the tricks we have been going through earlier can be used to manipulate history. But the real powerful and granular way to approach tweaking your local history is with the interactive rebase. Remember, if our history is local, we are free to tinker with it as we want. This capability gives us the opportunity and responsibility to consider the history we publish as a part of the delivery. The Git history that we deliver is also a form of communication, and it should be chopped up in the right commits in the right order, with good, clear commit messages. An interactive rebase is invoked by adding the flag `--interactive` to the git rebase command, for example, `git rebase --interactive master`.

The best way to go about preparing your Git history is the interactive rebase. Conceptually, you give Git a rebase target, which is what you want to rebase on top of. Then, Git provides you with a rebase plan that it intends to execute. You can change this plan, before Git executes it. This allows you to skip commits entirely, edit them, reorder them, or squash them together. The plan takes the form of **Action Sha**. And deleting a line will simply make the rebase skip that commit. If you do not edit the plan, it is the same as leaving out the --interactive flag on the rebase command.

The most common actions are as follows:

- **Pick** adds the commit at this point.
- **Squash** melds this commit into the previous commit.
- **Edit** stops to edit this commit.
- **Drop** does not pick this commit.

The preceding actions and reordering are how interactive rebases are most commonly used.

The following is an example rebase --interactive execution plan:

```
pick 8c1e4de file9
reword 921d2d0 file8
squash 3374035 file3
pick 5b3a4fc file4
pick f0d1634 file5
drop a7df72d file2
drop 3d7e5ea file6
pick 18bfdfe file7
```

The interactive rebase is perhaps the most powerful Git command, and almost any Git task can be solved using this command. I hope that becoming aware of this command will help you on your journey to always delivering a well-groomed history to your collaboration partners, and your future self.

Git Katas

To support the learning goals of this chapter, I suggest you do the following Git katas:

- Revert.

- Reset.

- Reorder the history.

- Then, I suggest you do the reset kata again; it is always a healthy exercise to revisit ☺.

Summary

Manipulating the history is often proclaimed to be a big no-no in version control because of traceability. But as long as we only rewrite history that is local or only has been published to temporary branches, we have the obligation to make the history the most usable it can be. Whether that is to squash multiple commits together or even split commits into different bundles, it is all about considering the history you deliver as part of your deliverable.

Remember, all the commands we have covered here are safe, and in the chapter on Git internals, we will cover how to recover from accidents.

CHAPTER 7

Customizing Git

Git is an engineer's tool, built by engineers. This means that while Git works a certain way out of the box, the real power is unleashed when we start customizing Git to match our way of working. With Git, we can do a lot in terms of simple configurations, creating shortcuts for the tasks that we often use, or have repository-specific configurations to help us manage the different contexts in which we work.

But Git does not stop there. Using hooks, we can inject scripts into the normal workflow of Git operations, to better support our workflows, and using Git attributes and filters, we can change the most basic operation of Git, how files are moved between the repository and the workspace. In this chapter, we will go through everything from the most basic configuration and alias to customization that changes some of the fundamental behaviors of Git.

Configuring Git

Git supports three levels of configurations: system, user, and repository local. In most scenarios, we only use the user configurations. System configurations are rarely used and could be used to some effect in multiuser environments to enforce some sane defaults. Repository local configurations are something that we as ordinary Git users could use to a much greater extent. Git applies configurations in the following order: system, user, and local. Each grouping overwrites any duplicate entries from the previous. This is illustrated in Figure 7-1.

© Johan Abildskov 2020
J. Abildskov, *Practical Git*, https://doi.org/10.1007/978-1-4842-6270-2_7

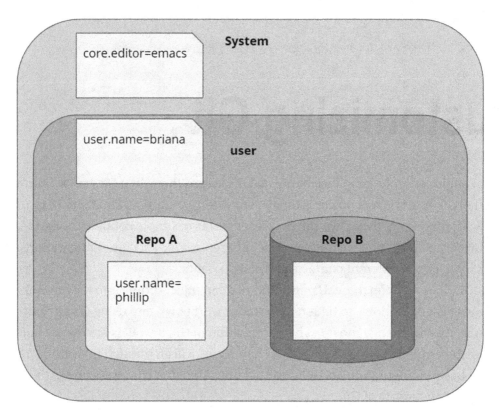

Figure 7-1. *In the global configuration, user.name is set to briana, while in Repo A, there is a .gitconfig file specifying user.name to be phillip. Thus, in global scope and Repo B, user.name will resolve to briana, while it will resolve to phillip in Repo A. In the system configuration, the default editor is set to emacs*

Applying configurations in Git is done through the interface git config. If we add --list to the command, we will read rather than set values. We use a key/value pair to set a configuration. Using the flags --global and `--system`, we can set user or system configurations, rather than the default repository local configurations. To set the pull strategy to always rebase for the current user, we would run the command `git config --global pull.rebase true`. If we rather wanted to set it for either the system, we would use --system, or to put it in the repository configuration, drop the `--global` flag. There are many configurations in Git, and we will not cover them here. Specific configurations can be found in the Git documentation. We will however cover Git configurations in the sense that they enable the next three sections.

GIT CONFIGURATION EXERCISE

In this exercise, we go through tweaking Git configurations. The repository for this exercise can be found in the exercises delivered with the book in the folder chapter7/.

In this exercise, we have two repositories config-ACME and config-AJAX that we are going to use to investigate how configurations overlap. First, we run the script setting up the exercise and then we can move on. Note, you might have issues running this in a non-bash prompt.

```
$ ./config.sh
$ cd config
$ ls
config-ACME/  config-AJAX/
$ git config user.email
randomsort@gmail.com
```

Here, we note that even though we are not in a Git repository, we have access to the configuration. Local configuration does not make any sense in this case. It is also unlikely that you will get the same email returned as I do.

```
$ cd config-ACME
$ git config user.email
janedoe@acme
```

Entering the ACME repository, we can see that the user's email is now different. We access the local and global scope to verify the source of this configuration.

```
$ git config --local user.email
janedoe@acme
$ git config --global user.email
randomsort@gmail.com
```

We can also obtain the same information with the flag --show-origin.

```
$ git config --show-origin user.email
file:.git/config         janedoe@acme
```

Now, we go to the other repository to see what values we get.

```
$ cd ..
$ cd config-AJAX/
$ git config user.email
```

```
randomsort@gmail.com
$ git config --local user.email
$ git config --show-origin user.email
file:C:/Users/Rando/.gitconfig   randomsort@gmail.com
```

In this repository, we notice that the local user.email is not set, so we access the user defined instead. We verify this using --show-origin.

The user.email configuration is a part of Git out of the box, but we can also add arbitrary configurations for our own purposes. In these repositories, we are working with a custom configuration that we have called practical-git. We can have multiple entries in our sections, each with a name, but we are working with the company key.

```
cd ../config-ACME
$ git config practical-git.company
ACME
In the ACME repository company contains the value ACME, let's check in AJAX.
$ cd ../config-AJAX/
$ git config  practical-git.company
UNKNOWN
```

Here, we receive the value UNKNOWN, so let's set the configuration to AJAX.

```
$ git config practical-git.company AJAX
$ git config practical-git.company
AJAX
We can still access the global scope.
$ git config --global practical-git.company
UNKNOWN
```

Now that we have contaminated your global configuration space with this section, we will delete this section to remove this from your configuration file.

```
$ git config --remove-section --global practical-git
$ git config --get --global practical-git.company
```

This concludes the exercise. We have gone through the user and local scope and how you can have different configurations in different repositories. This can be particularly useful if you use the same computer to personal, open source, and company projects.

Aliases

In Git, we can use aliases to construct shortcuts or extend Git's functionality. We can either use commands that are native to Git or invoke external commands. A frequent target for aliases is making your logs aligned perfectly with your particular tastes. My go-to log command is `git log --oneline --decorate --graph --all` which is a long string to type, leaving ample room for typos and other errors. Commonly, I am unable to spell `--oneline` correctly. In this scenario, I could create an alias for that command. There is no direct alias command, but we can use git config to set aliases. Note that this also means that we can have differently scoped aliases.

GIT ALIAS EXERCISE

In this exercise, we are going to set up some aliases for common tasks in our repository. The repository for this exercise can be found in `chapter7/aliases`.

I often use a rather long variation of log to investigate repositories.

```
$ git log --decorate --oneline --graph --all
$ git log --decorate --oneline --graph --all
* b5566ae (myBranch) 7
* 506bb29 6
* f662f41 5
* bd90c39 (HEAD -> master) 5
* 55936c5 4
* 6519696 3
| * e645e36 (newBranch) 9
| * d5ed404 8
|/
* 0425411 (tag: originalVersion) 2
* 11fbef7 1
```

Of course, this is tedious and often leads to typos and my not remembering what parts I actually want to add. So let us set up an alias for this command. We set up all the aliases in the local repository so we do not leak into our global scope.

```
$ git config --local alias.l "log --oneline --decorate --graph --all"
This allows us to use git l as a shortcut to the longer variation.
$ git l
$ git log --decorate --oneline --graph --all
* b5566ae (myBranch) 7
* 506bb29 6
* f662f41 5
* bd90c39 (HEAD -> master) 5
* 55936c5 4
* 6519696 3
| * e645e36 (newBranch) 9
| * d5ed404 8
|/
* 0425411 (tag: originalVersion) 2
* 11fbef7 1
```

Already a bunch of keystrokes have been spared, and we are optimizing our way of working. Next up, we will add a shortcut to running an external command. In this simple case, we will simply execute `ls -al`, but it could be an arbitrarily complex command. Note that we add an exclamation mark at the beginning of the alias to signal that it is not a Git command we are running. This can be useful for extending Git. This is, for instance, how Git LFS started. Consider if you would be better off doing a shell alias.

```
$ git config --local alias.ll '!ls -al'

$ git ll
total 10
drwxr-xr-x 1 joab 1049089   0 Jul  9 13:10 .
drwxr-xr-x 1 joab 1049089   0 Jul  9 13:10 ..
drwxr-xr-x 1 joab 1049089   0 Jul  9 13:14 .git
-rw-r--r-- 1 joab 1049089 155 Jul  9 13:10 gitconfig-alias
-rw-r--r-- 1 joab 1049089  25 Jul  9 13:10 test
So now we have augmented Git's functionality ever so slightly.
We can all set up scripts to run as in the following section.
$ git config --local alias.helloworld '!f() { echo "Hello World"; }; f'
joab@LT02920 MINGW64 ~/repos/randomsort/practical-git/chapter7/aliases (master)
$ git helloworld
Hello World
```

And we can make our scripts take arguments.

```
$ git config --local alias.helloperson '!f() { echo "Hello, ${1}"; }; f'
$ git helloperson Phillip
Hello, Phillip
```

While these aliases are simple, they should show how powerful a tool they are and how you can both make shortcuts for your often-used commands and extend Git with additional functionality. If you have a common set of things you do in your workflow, you can create aliases for each of these and share them with your team. It is a good way to align on your way of working.

As we have seen, we can quickly create shortcuts for custom commands or even substitute complex parts of our workflow with an alias. Aliases are a massively underused Git feature when it comes to ordinary developers. From now on, you are obligated to create aliases for those things you find yourselves typing out often. You might also once in a while need a complex piece of magic, and the next time you do so, create an alias for it, so it will always be ready at hand.

Attributes

Git attributes are a somewhat advanced part of Git's feature set. It is one of the places where we can fundamentally change the way Git writes objects in its internal database. They are commonly used to enforce line endings or how to handle binary files, but can also be used to convert to specific coding styles on check-in. As this is something that happens client-side, if we truly want to enforce anything, we need to implement it server-side or in automation engines.

The way we implement attributes is in a .gitignore-like fashion. We create .gitattributes files, and in those, we list paths on which we set and unset attributes on these particular paths. If, for instance, we want to let Git know that a particular XML file is autogenerated and should never be merged like a text file, we can set the attribute binary on it, leading to a .gitattributes like so:

```
autogeneratedFile.xml binary
```

Setting the -text attribute on a path stops Git from treating matching paths as text files. The most common scenarios for tweaking existing Git behavior come from either removing the text behavior as shown earlier or forcing Git to treat line endings in a particular way.

We can also use Git attributes to add functionality that is disconnected from what Git would otherwise do. We can do this by adding filters to our configs and reference those filters from our `.gitattributes`. Git LFS (Git Large File Storage) uses this to handle large files. Filters change how Git handles files going in and how of the repository. Git LFS uploads the matching paths to a central binary repository manager and only saves the reference in Git on check-in. On checkout, Git LFS resolves those paths and downloads the binary files. Git LFS seemingly allows us to store large binary files in Git, which Git is notoriously bad at handling. This reduction in repository size comes at the cost of being able to work fully offline. Not being able to work entirely distributed can be a problem if connectivity is a sparse resource in your context. This filter workflow is shown in Figure 7-2.

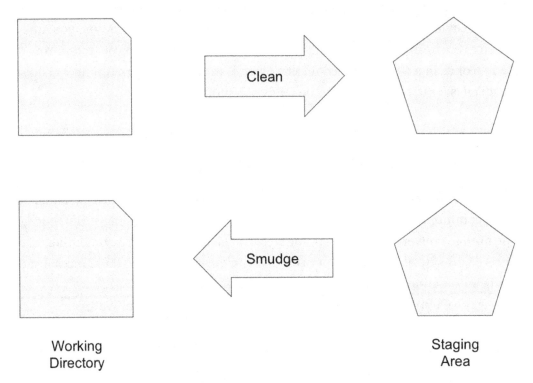

Figure 7-2. The clean filter applies when going from the working directory to the staging area and the other direction for smudge

In my experience, Git attributes are rarely necessary unless you have some complexity in your context, such as multiple different platforms on which you check out code using tools that are fragile when it comes to line endings. Of course, the right solution is to fix the fragility or complexity, but until then, Git attributes can help work around the problems.

ATTRIBUTES

In this exercise, we are going to go through a previous kata that generated a merge conflict for us and investigate how we can use .gitattributes to change what happens. In this exercise, we are going to go through the kata merge-mergesort, because we know that will make a merge conflict happen and we can change the outcome of this using Git attributes.

```
$ cd merge-mergesort
$ . setup.sh
```

Now, we are in the exercise and we can force the merge conflict by merging in the branch Mergesort-Impl.

```
$ git merge Mergesort-Impl
Auto-merging mergesort.py
CONFLICT (content): Merge conflict in mergesort.py
Automatic merge failed; fix conflicts and then commit the result.
$ git status
On branch master
You have unmerged paths.
  (fix conflicts and run "git commit")
  (use "git merge --abort" to abort the merge)
Unmerged paths:
  (use "git add <file>..." to mark resolution)
        both modified:   mergesort.py
no changes added to commit (use "git add" and/or "git commit -a")

$ cat mergesort.py
from heapq import merge

def merge_sort2(m):
    """Sort list, using two part merge sort"""
    if len(m) <= 1:
        return m

    # Determine the pivot point
    middle = len(m) // 2

    # Split the list at the pivot
<<<<<<< HEAD
```

```
        left = m[:middle]
        right = m[middle:]
=======
        right = m[middle:]
        left = m[:middle]
>>>>>>> Mergesort-Impl
        # Sort recursively
        right = merge_sort2(right)
        left = merge_sort2(left)
        # Merge and return
        return list(merge(right, left))

def merge_sort4(m):
    """Sort list, using four part merge sort"""
    if len(m) <= 4:
        return sorted(m)

    # Determine the pivot point
    middle = len(m) // 2
    leftMiddle = middle // 2
    rightMiddle = middle + leftMiddle

    # Split the list at the pivots
    first = m[:leftMiddle]
    second = m[leftMiddle:middle]
    third = m[middle:rightMiddle]
<<<<<<< HEAD
    last = m[rightMiddle:]
=======
    fourth = m[rightMiddle:]
>>>>>>> Mergesort-Impl

    # Sort recursively
    first = merge_sort4(first)
    second = merge_sort4(second)
    third = merge_sort4(third)
<<<<<<< HEAD
    last = merge_sort4(last)
```

```
    # Merge and return
    return list(merge(first, second, third, last))
=======
    fourth = merge_sort4(fourth)

    # Merge and return
    return list(merge(first,second, third, fourth))
>>>>>>> Mergesort-Impl
```

In the preceding code, we notice that there are merge markers. This would have been bad if it had been an autogenerated file or a file where merging doesn't make any sense. So we abandon the merge.

```
$ git merge --abort
We then make Git consider mergesort.py a binary file, not to be automatically
merged. We then repeat the merge.
$ echo "mergesort.py binary" > .gitattributes
$ git merge Mergesort-Impl
warning: Cannot merge binary files: mergesort.py (HEAD vs. Mergesort-Impl)
Auto-merging mergesort.py
CONFLICT (content): Merge conflict in mergesort.py
Automatic merge failed; fix conflicts and then commit the result.
$ cat mergesort.py
from heapq import merge

def merge_sort2(m):
    """Sort list, using two part merge sort"""
    if len(m) <= 1:
        return m

    # Determine the pivot point
    middle = len(m) // 2

    # Split the list at the pivot
    left = m[:middle]
    right = m[middle:]

    # Sort recursively
    right = merge_sort2(right)
    left = merge_sort2(left)
```

```python
    # Merge and return
    return list(merge(right, left))

def merge_sort4(m):
    """Sort list, using four part merge sort"""
    if len(m) <= 4:
        return sorted(m)

    # Determine the pivot point
    middle = len(m) // 2
    leftMiddle = middle // 2
    rightMiddle = middle + leftMiddle

    # Split the list at the pivots
    first = m[:leftMiddle]
    second = m[leftMiddle:middle]
    third = m[middle:rightMiddle]
    last = m[rightMiddle:]

    # Sort recursively
    first = merge_sort4(first)
    second = merge_sort4(second)
    third = merge_sort4(third)
    last = merge_sort4(last)

    # Merge and return
    return list(merge(first, second, third, last))
```

As we can see, we no longer have merge markers in our file but rather have one large self-contained file. We can use git checkout with the flags --ours and --theirs to establish either the incoming file or the one already present in our branch.

```
$ git checkout --ours -- mergesort.py
$ git add mergesort.py
$ git commit -m "merge"
$ git status
```

On branch master

Untracked files:

```
  (use "git add <file>..." to include in what will be committed)
        .gitattributes
```

nothing added to commit but untracked files present (use "git add" to track)

So we resolved the merge nicely. If we already know which source we want if there are any conflicts, we can specify that as a merge strategy as a flag to the merge command. First, we reset to the previous stage and then repeat the merge with the strategy flag.

```
$ git reset --hard HEAD~1
HEAD is now at b4cac37 Mergesort implemented on master
$ git merge --strategy ours Mergesort-Impl
Merge made by the 'ours' strategy.
```

This exercise showed a simple way to use Git attributes to change the way Git works. There are more advanced things to do with Git attributes, but they are beyond the scope of this book.

Diff and Merge Tools

While the command-line or IDE extensions are enough for most use cases, there are situations where your domain sets you up for some challenging diffs and merges. If this is the case, we can configure Git to use external tools to handle this. Perhaps unsurprising, we set up the tools in git config and can then invoke them through the command line. The process is similar for merge and diff tools. If we have configured a diff tool, we can invoke it through git difftool, and if we have configured a merge tool, the command is git mergetool. There are both free, open source, and proprietary merge tools available. We are using the open source tool meld in the exercise, while a popular paid tool is BeyondCompare. Your team or department might have a preferred tool. If so, it is a good idea to align on that.

MERGE TOOL

This exercise assumes that you have installed the meld merge tool (meldmerge.com) and that you are on Windows. If you are on a different platform, I recommend you follow the platform-specific guides for configuring meld and mergetools, but you will likely have an easier time than those on Windows. First, we will configure meld as the mergetool, and then we will revisit the merge-mergesort kata to see how the merge looks when we use a merge tool to resolve the conflict.

When I installed Meld, it wound up in the path C:\Program Files (x86)\Meld\meld.exe, so I want to point Git to that.

```
$ git config --global mergetool.meld.path 'C:\Program Files (x86)\Meld\Meld.exe'
```

Then, we can tell Git to use Meld as mergetool and difftool.

```
$ git config --global merge.tool meld
$ git config --global diff.tool meld
So let's go back to the merge-mergesort kata. Remember to run the setup
script again to get a clean kata.
$ pwd
$ . setup.sh
$ git diff Mergesort-Impl
diff --git a/mergesort.py b/mergesort.py
index 9de927a..646b20f 100644
--- a/mergesort.py
+++ b/mergesort.py
@@ -9,8 +9,8 @@ def merge_sort2(m):
     middle = len(m) // 2

     # Split the list at the pivot
-    right = m[middle:]
     left = m[:middle]
+    right = m[middle:]

     # Sort recursively
     right = merge_sort2(right)
@@ -33,13 +33,13 @@ def merge_sort4(m):
     first = m[:leftMiddle]
     second = m[leftMiddle:middle]
```

```
      third = m[middle:rightMiddle]
-     fourth = m[rightMiddle:]
+     last = m[rightMiddle:]

      # Sort recursively
      first = merge_sort4(first)
      second = merge_sort4(second)
      third = merge_sort4(third)
-     fourth = merge_sort4(fourth)
+     last = merge_sort4(last)

      # Merge and return
-     return list(merge(first,second, third, fourth))
+     return list(merge(first, second, third, last))
```

This diff could be useless for more complex products. And we can run meld using the difftool command.

```
$ git difftool Mergesort-impl
```

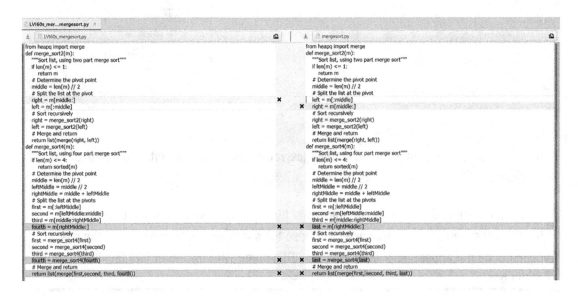

Now, we have a more visual view.

Let's try to move on with the merge.

```
$ git merge Mergesort-Impl
Auto-merging mergesort.py
CONFLICT (content): Merge conflict in mergesort.py
```

133

Automatic merge failed; fix conflicts and then commit the result.

```
$ git mergetool
Merging:
mergesort.py
Normal merge conflict for 'mergesort.py':
  {local}: modified file
  {remote}: modified file
```

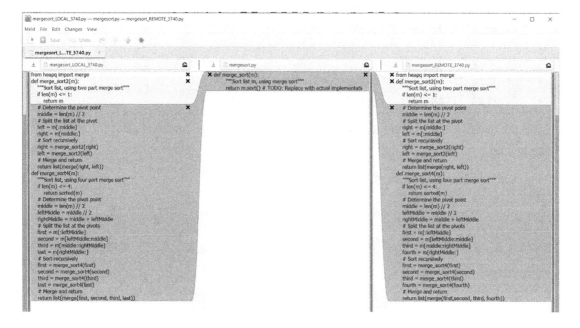

So, we get a visual way of resolving our merges, rather than *manually* setting the state of the conflicted path.

This can be useful if you work with particular file types or have complex merge conflicts, but I rarely encounter an actual need for these tools in practice. In most cases, the merge conflicts do not appear, and when they do, IDEs come with excellent tool facilitation out of the box.

Hooks

The final configuration option that we cover is Git hooks. Hooks are small shell scripts that allow us to inject functionality in the flow of Git actions. Hooks can help prevent us doing things that we shouldn't or prepare data for Git.

Hooks are available server-side and client-side. In this book, we only cover client-side hooks, but if you ever notice that a server rejects a push because of non-fast-forward merges, you have seen a server-side hook in action. Other often-used server-side hooks check for a referenced issue or prevent you from accidentally adding large files to your repository.

When it comes to client-side hooks, the same phrase that I've used many times is still valid. You can only support workflows client-side if you want to enforce anything you have to do in server-side. Hooks reside in the folder .git/hooks, and when you git init a repository, there is a set of sample hooks that you can check out to see examples of Git hooks in action. If hooks exit with a nonzero exit code, the current action is aborted. We use this in the next exercise to prevent commits on the master branch using the pre-commit hook. In the case of the prepare-commit-msg hook, we can both check for something, that is, the presence of curse words in the commit message or the lack of a referenced issue ID. Thus, hooks help us do the right thing, and through the path of least resistance, we improve. We can, of course, circumvent this locally. Note that hooks are not shared across distributed repositories as this would pose a security issue.

GIT HOOK EXERCISE

In this exercise, we have gone through how to implement a simple hook helping us avoid a common mistake and how to circumvent that hook when we need to. This repository for this exercise can be found in the folder chapter7/pre-commit-hook. If you are on a Mac and experience issues, you can look at this Stack Overflow post for assistance: https://stackoverflow.com/a/14219160/28376.

```
$ ls
pre-commit*
```

We can see there is a single file here, but let's first check that we are able to create a commit in normal fashion.

```
$ echo "test" > testfile.txt
```

```
$ git add testfile.txt
$ git commit -m "Initial commit"
[master (root-commit) 8d6ae42] Initial commit
 1 file changed, 1 insertion(+)
  create mode 100644 testfile.txt
```

Nothing surprising here, we could stage a file and create a commit. So let's look at the content in the file pre-commit. You do not have to be a shell ninja to be able to discern the structure of this script. We exit with an error with the current branch is master; otherwise, we exit with zero. There are a few echo statements to let us see the control flow.

```
$ cat pre-commit
#!/bin/bash

echo "Running Hook"

if [ `git rev-parse --abbrev-ref HEAD` = master ]
then
    echo "You can't commit to master"
    exit 1
else
    echo "Commit freely on this branch"
fi
```

Hooks are active by being in the .git/hooks folder and having a name matching when it should run. Our hook is called pre-commit, so it will run before a commit is created.

```
$ cp pre-commit .git/hooks
```

With our hook now in place, we will try to see if we can create an additional commit.

```
$ echo "more content" >> testfile.txt
$ git commit -am "Add more content"
Running Hook
You can't commit to master
```

Our commit gets rejected, so we will make another branch and create the commit here.

```
$ git checkout -b other
Switched to a new branch 'other'

$ git commit -am "Add more content"
Running Hook
```

```
Commit freely on this branch
[other ec31264] Add more content
 1 file changed, 1 insertion(+)
```

Our hook runs, but as we are on a different branch, the commit is allowed through. This can be useful to way those oops moments.

But let us say that we really do want to commit on master, even though there is a hook preventing us from doing so. Let's go back to master and create a commit there.

```
$ git checkout master
$ echo "some items of interest" > test
$ git add test
$ git commit -m "on master"
Running Hook
You can't commit to master
```

Our hook is still working and stopping us from committing to master. However, we can prevent the hook from running using the flag --no-verify.

```
$ git commit --no-verify -am "on master"
[master c6d4486] on master
 1 file changed, 1 insertion(+)
 create mode 100644 test
```

This is the reason that I have been saying that we need to handle enforcement server-side. One might argue that --no-verify is a bad practice, or couldn't we just disable it? But consider that the hooks reside in the local repository and there is nothing hindering the user from simply deleting the hook altogether.

At least `--no-verify` provides us with a proper way to skip the hook.

Katas

To support the learning goals in this chapter, I suggest you practice the following katas:

- Git-attributes

- Pre-push

To supplement this, you can go into any local Git repository and look at the sample hooks in the `.git/hooks` folder.

Summary

In this chapter, we covered many different ways that you can customize your Git installation to work more efficiently and support arbitrary workflows and constraints.

We covered how config files allow us to have global, user, and repository local configurations and how we could use those configurations to extend Git functionality.

We built our own shortcuts and called external commands using aliases. We investigate Git attributes and how we could use them to both tweak Git's default performance and completely change the base functionality of Git. We covered how you can get a custom merging experience using mergetools. Finally, we covered how we can interfere in the standard Git Flow using hooks to facilitate our workflows.

CHAPTER 8

Additional Git Features

In this chapter, I have a lovely amalgam of Git features for you – features that I could not find any place to put. The reason they ended up here might be that where they would have originally fit, we had not established the right mental models, or that they are slightly tangential to the rest of the content in this book. These are features that might help you in your work but should not come into play on an everyday basis. Being aware of their existence might key you in for those dire situations where they are just the right thing for you. We cover figuring out what specific commit introduced a discrepancy using Git bisect. We use Git Submodules to manage dependencies between repositories. And we are going to use Git Large File Storage or Git LFS for short. If you made it this far, congratulations. You have completed the Practical Git curriculum and mastered the foundations. The rest is the icing on the cake.

Git Bisect

In a perfect world, we have quick tests that we can run on every commit, letting us know if we introduce an error, breaking existing functionality. Unfortunately, this seems to be a utopic vision. In reality, we seldom have perfect tests, and even when we do have extensive test coverage, there are no guarantees that no bugs slip through our net. It can also be a nonbreaking change, such as an element changing the color, which would have been hard to test for in a meaningful way. In these cases, we can revert the change manually, to remedy the unwanted change. But this is both tedious and error-prone. Plus, there might be a good reason for this change to be valid. As such, it is valuable to be able to find the commit that introduced the change.

The most straightforward strategy is to start from the most recent commit that was in a healthy state and check out commits one at a time. For each commit, poke around and figure out if it was the commit that introduced the test. At some point, we figure out the commit that introduced the breaking change, and we can revert that

© Johan Abildskov 2020
J. Abildskov, *Practical Git*, https://doi.org/10.1007/978-1-4842-6270-2_8

commit. If we are lucky, we have tests that we can run in each commit to verify the quality of the given commit. Worst-case scenario, we need to check all of the commits between the good and the bad commit, and it is a tiresome and arduous task. This linear strategy is in Figure 8-1. There can be small improvements such as starting from the newest commit if you believe it was a recent change you are looking for, but nevertheless, it might take a long time.

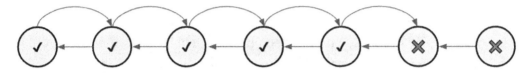

Figure 8-1. *Searching through history in a linear fashion*

We are fortunate that Git provides us with a better way of finding the culprit. You might have heard of *binary search*. Binary is a superior approach to finding an element in a sorted list. As we are searching through time, we can consider our commit history to be a sorted list. Binary search is recursively looking at the middle element to determine if the desired element is in the left or right half of the list. When we keep doing this, it quickly yields the desired element. The performance is particularly attractive for long histories. Looking through 1000 elements linearly takes a long time and has a horrible worst case of going through all the elements. Using binary search, we can guarantee that we have found the element after at most 11 iterations. This is a huge difference! Figure 8-2 shows jumping through history to find the breaking change.

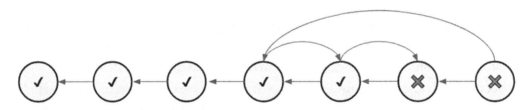

Figure 8-2. *Jumping through the history like a binary search*

It is tedious to keep track of where we are and what commit to investigate. Git instruments this with the command bisect.

Git bisect works by marking a commit as being bad and one as being good. Then, bisect will iteratively check out commits that we can mark as either good or bad, and bisect will continue until it is unambiguous which commit was the first bad one.

GIT BISECT EXERCISE

In this exercise, we will go through the bisect kata. It can be found in the katas repository in the bisect folder. In this exercise, we are left with 100 commits and changes in 50 files. It's no easy task to figure out when this broke! Fortunately, we have a script that can verify if a commit is broken, so we will use bisect to move through history.

```
$ . setup.sh
<Truncated>

$ git bisect start
```

After having started the bisection, we need to mark a commit as good and one as bad. This sets the endpoints for our search. We find the tag that we want to mark as good and mark HEAD as bad.

```
$ git tag
initial-commit

$ git bisect good initial-commit

$ git bisect bad
Bisecting: 49 revisions left to test after this (roughly 6 steps)
[9d7c0188ea01453068cab551cd07bc2f52cb4a44] 50
```

Now that we have marked the endpoints for the search, Git checks out the first commit that we need to verify. We use the script test.sh in the exercise folder to verify the commit. Depending on the test outcome, we mark the commit as either good or bad and continues verifying the commits that Git presents us with.

```
$ ./test.sh
test failed

$ git bisect bad
Bisecting: 24 revisions left to test after this (roughly 5 steps)
[7ff73ce2a82182eaa46e7239e093b976b851c2fc] 25

$ ./test.sh
test failed

$ git bisect bad
Bisecting: 12 revisions left to test after this (roughly 4 steps)
[1bb261b8f8d9549430af7c93e27c54a25abee63d] 12
```

```
$ ./test.sh
test passed

$ git bisect good
Bisecting: 6 revisions left to test after this (roughly 3 steps)
[c3b042dd17d10492c94d2544ec36982637efef36] 18

$ ./test.sh
test passed

$ git bisect good
Bisecting: 3 revisions left to test after this (roughly 2 steps)
[a604e7c7d423c6271925d1f7431cdbaa0c069a5a] 21

$ ./test.sh
test passed

$ git bisect good
Bisecting: 1 revision left to test after this (roughly 1 step)
[878630d3e906eb6e262f58d16b5611c79313ba91] 23

$ ./test.sh
test failed

$ git bisect bad
Bisecting: 0 revisions left to test after this (roughly 0 steps)
[819fa50314086a1e031427704e7bbc9419375cfd] 22

$ ./test.sh
test failed

$ git bisect bad
819fa50314086a1e031427704e7bbc9419375cfd is the first bad commit
commit 819fa50314086a1e031427704e7bbc9419375cfd
Author: Johan Abildskov <randomsort@gmail.com>
Date:   Sun Aug 2 21:15:32 2020 +0200

    22

 22.txt | 0
 1 file changed, 0 insertions(+), 0 deletions(-)
 create mode 100644 22.txt
```

While this was tedious, we unambiguously found the bad commit and with a good guarantee on the maximum amount of commits that we need to test.

Fortunately, because we were provided with a test, we can do this even more efficiently using git bisect run.

```
$ git bisect reset
Previous HEAD position was 819fa50 22
Switched to branch 'master'

$ git bisect start

$ git bisect good initial-commit

$ git bisect bad
Bisecting: 49 revisions left to test after this (roughly 6 steps)
[9d7c0188ea01453068cab551cd07bc2f52cb4a44] 50
```

After the Git provides us with the initial commit to verify, rather than doing so manually, we pass the test script to bisect.

```
$ git bisect run './test.sh'
running ./test.sh
test failed
Bisecting: 24 revisions left to test after this (roughly 5 steps)
[7ff73ce2a82182eaa46e7239e093b976b851c2fc] 25
running ./test.sh
test failed
Bisecting: 12 revisions left to test after this (roughly 4 steps)
[1bb261b8f8d9549430af7c93e27c54a25abee63d] 12
running ./test.sh
test passed
Bisecting: 6 revisions left to test after this (roughly 3 steps)
[c3b042dd17d10492c94d2544ec36982637efef36] 18
running ./test.sh
test passed
Bisecting: 3 revisions left to test after this (roughly 2 steps)
[a604e7c7d423c6271925d1f7431cdbaa0c069a5a] 21
running ./test.sh
test passed
Bisecting: 1 revision left to test after this (roughly 1 step)
```

```
[878630d3e906eb6e262f58d16b5611c79313ba91] 23
running ./test.sh
test failed
Bisecting: 0 revisions left to test after this (roughly 0 steps)
[819fa50314086a1e031427704e7bbc9419375cfd] 22
running ./test.sh
test failed
819fa50314086a1e031427704e7bbc9419375cfd is the first bad commit
commit 819fa50314086a1e031427704e7bbc9419375cfd
Author: Johan Abildskov <randomsort@gmail.com>
Date:   Sun Aug 2 21:15:32 2020 +0200

    22

 22.txt | 0
 1 file changed, 0 insertions(+), 0 deletions(-)
 create mode 100644 22.txt
bisect run success
```

Using run, we found the offending commit easily. In many cases, it will pay off to have. This exercise showed how we could smoothly go about figuring out the particular commit that introduced a given change or bug.

Git bisect is an excellent feature, but it requires you to care about the history that you create. If you create bundle too many changes into a single commit, then it will still be difficult to figure out what particular part of that commit introduced the bad change. Ideally, you would be able to revert the bad commit as the change was atomic. Git bisect also is easier to work with when you do not have many merges and levels of branches. As such it can be easier to work with bisect, if you are using rebase, rather than merges.

Git Submodules

One of the general problems in developing software is handling dependencies and using code from other people. Whether this code is open sourced and publicly available or proprietary, how you get that code into your workspace in a traceable manner is a challenge. Depending on the ecosystem of your programming language of choice, there are preferred solutions. Python has pip packages, JavaScript npm, and .NET NuGet packages, and many languages have their own. The native package management should be the preferred solution for sharing code across code bases. In some scenarios, such a solution might not present itself. C and C++ do not come with a native dependency management solution, for instance. In these scenarios, we can turn to Git Submodules to share code across code bases. As Git is language-agnostic, it should be our fallback solution rather than the default. Defaulting to Git Submodules for dependency management causes you to miss out on the benefits of the integrated ecosystem.

With Git Submodules, we add folders whose content should come from a different repository. Git Submodules uses a file called .gitmodules to keep track of paths that are submodules. This allows Git to restore the content of that folder to what we remote we have added. If, for instance, we want to add the Git katas repository as a dependency in our repository, we can run the command git submodule add git@github.com:eficode-academy/git-katas katas. After running this command, the folder katas contains the content of the master branch on the kata repositorycc. If we look at the content of .gitmodules, it looks as follows.

Listing 8-1. Content of .gitmodules after adding submodule

```
$ cat .gitmodules
[submodule "katas"]
        path = katas
        url = git@github.com:eficode-academy/git-katas
```

Note that this is very different from putting the katas repository manually inside another Git repo, which is something we should never do. The `.gitmodules` file allows us to reestablish this dependency in other clones of our remote. Git Submodule configuration lives in `.git/config`, but as that is not shared across remotes, we need to initialize submodules to re-create the configuration from `.gitmodules` on new clones. This initialization is either done by `git submodule init`, followed by `git submodule update`, or `git submodule update --init`. The latter is preferred unless you need to customize submodule locations. Init restores configuration to `.git/config`, while update checks out the content to the path.

Note   One of the challenges of working with submodules is keeping track on which project you are currently trying to make a change in. Is this a change on the outer or inner project? There is no way to help with this, other than being deliberate about what changes belong where and focusing while delivering.

SUBMODULE EXERCISE

In this exercise, we go through the Git Submodule kata. We show how to add submodules and the workflow around delivering changes to both outer and inner repositories. The submodule kata is in the katas in the folder submodules/.

First, we set up the exercise.

```
cd submodules/
$ ls
README.md  setup.ps1  setup.sh
$ . setup.sh
<Truncated>
$ ls
component  product  remote
```

We note three folders, each a Git repository. We have the product that we are building. The folder remote represents the presence of the component on a repository manager like GitHub. The component folder represents the local working folder of those developing the submodule.

The first thing we do is add the component to our product.

```
$ cd product/

/product$ ls
product.h

/product$ git submodule add ../remote include
Cloning into '/home/randomsort/repos/git-katas/submodules/exercise/product/
include'...
done.
/product$ ls
include  product.h
/product$ git status
On branch master
Changes to be committed:
  (use "git reset HEAD <file>..." to unstage)

        new file:   .gitmodules
        new file:   include
```

We observe that the two paths have changed: the .gitmodules file that keeps track of submodules and the path where we have added the submodule.

Inside include, the content of the module is present.

```
/product$ ls include
component.h
/product$ cd include
/product/include$ git status
On branch master
Your branch is up to date with 'origin/master'.

nothing to commit, working tree clean
```

The status of the submodule is clean, even though our root repository is dirty. This is one of the things that can be tricky with submodules.

```
/product/include$ cd ..
/product$ git diff --cached
diff --git a/.gitmodules b/.gitmodules
new file mode 100644
index 0000000..79d5c92
--- /dev/null
+++ b/.gitmodules
@@ -0,0 +1,3 @@
+[submodule "include"]
+       path = include
+       url = ../remote
diff --git a/include b/include
new file mode 160000
index 0000000..3aecaf4
--- /dev/null
+++ b/include
@@ -0,0 +1 @@
+Subproject commit 3aecaf441cca7d98cbec906bf7bf61902fcd41ee
```

The diff in the product repository matches what we expect based on the previous step, except for the +Subproject commit <hash> line.

```
/product$ cat .gitmodules
[submodule "include"]
        path = include
        url = ../remote
```

However, when we look in the .gitmodules file, there is no information letting us know which commit we have added to our product repository. This is because Git is storing that object reference directly in its internal database as a commit listing in its tree object. We cover how commits are constructed and how trees look like in the next chapter.

Now, we commit our change to the product repository, namely, adding the submodule.

```
/product$ git commit -m "Add component"
[master f7a101d] Add component
 2 files changed, 4 insertions(+)
 create mode 100644 .gitmodules
 create mode 160000 include
/product$ cd ..
```

Let's move on and create a change inside of the submodules remote. As the submodule itself is a completely ordinary Git repository, nothing new is going on here.

```
$ cd component
/component$ ls
component.h
/component$ git status
On branch master
Your branch is up to date with 'origin/master'.

nothing to commit, working tree clean
/component$ echo "important change" > file
/component$ git add file
/component$ git commit -m "important change"
[master 19451c0] important change
 1 file changed, 1 insertion(+)
 create mode 100644 file
/component$ git status
On branch master
Your branch is ahead of 'origin/master' by 1 commit.
  (use "git push" to publish your local commits)
```

```
nothing to commit, working tree clean
/component$ git push
Counting objects: 3, done.
Delta compression using up to 4 threads.
Compressing objects: 100% (2/2), done.
Writing objects: 100% (3/3), 298 bytes | 149.00 KiB/s, done.
Total 3 (delta 0), reused 0 (delta 0)
To /home/randomsort/repos/git-katas/submodules/exercise/remote
   3aecaf4..19451c0  master -> master
/component$ cd ..
```

We published the change to the remote. Let's check how that looks from the perspective of the product.

```
$ cd product
/product$ git status
On branch master
nothing to commit, working tree clean
```

Our master branch is clean, so we do not detect a change of the submodule.

```
/product$ git submodule foreach 'git status'
Entering 'include'
On branch master
Your branch is up to date with 'origin/master'.

nothing to commit, working tree clean
```

Even going through the submodules and running status in there does not help us. We need to pull inside of the submodule.

```
/product$ cd include
/product/include$ git pull
remote: Counting objects: 3, done.
remote: Compressing objects: 100% (2/2), done.
remote: Total 3 (delta 0), reused 0 (delta 0)
Unpacking objects: 100% (3/3), done.
From /home/randomsort/repos/git-katas/submodules/exercise/remote
   3aecaf4..19451c0  master      -> origin/master
Updating 3aecaf4..19451c0
Fast-forward
```

```
 file | 1 +
 1 file changed, 1 insertion(+)
 create mode 100644 file
/product/include$ ls
component.h  file
```

While this works and we could have used `git submodule foreach` to iterate over each of our repositories, it becomes less transparent what changes we are pulling into our product.

```
/product/include$ cd ..
/product$ git status
On branch master
Changes not staged for commit:
  (use "git add <file>..." to update what will be committed)
  (use "git checkout -- <file>..." to discard changes in working directory)

        modified:   include (new commits)

no changes added to commit (use "git add" and/or "git commit -a")
```

After updating the submodule, we can see that there is a change from the vantage point of the product. With git diff, we can see the change from tracking one commit to another. We commit that change to our product.

```
/product$ git diff
diff --git a/include b/include
index 3aecaf4..19451c0 160000
--- a/include
+++ b/include
@@ -1 +1 @@
-Subproject commit 3aecaf441cca7d98cbec906bf7bf61902fcd41ee
+Subproject commit 19451c07652a282a71eeb7d953d9d807c66284a8

/product$ git add .
/product$ git commit -m "Update include"
[master ebb028e] Update include
 1 file changed, 1 insertion(+), 1 deletion(-)
```

With the product thus updated, we can take advantage of having the submodule embedded as a proper Git repository inside of our product. This is a powerful feature as we can develop our submodule in the context of the product that uses it. It has the disadvantage that it becomes more difficult to discern when you are working in which repository, and if a submodule is used in multiple products, it is unlikely to be a good idea to develop in the context of a single specific product.

```
/product$ cd include/
/product/include$ ls
component.h  file
/product/include$ git mv file file.txt
/product/include$ git status
On branch master
Your branch is up to date with 'origin/master'.

Changes to be committed:
  (use "git reset HEAD <file>..." to unstage)

        renamed:    file -> file.txt

/product/include$ git commit -m "Add file extension to file"
[master d9ba324] Add file extension to file
 1 file changed, 0 insertions(+), 0 deletions(-)
 rename file => file.txt (100%)
/product/include$ git push
Counting objects: 2, done.
Delta compression using up to 4 threads.
Compressing objects: 100% (2/2), done.
Writing objects: 100% (2/2), 285 bytes | 285.00 KiB/s, done.
Total 2 (delta 0), reused 0 (delta 0)
To /home/randomsort/repos/git-katas/submodules/exercise/remote
   19451c0..d9ba324  master -> master
```

We have delivered a change to the submodule from the Git repository embedded in our product. Next, we clone a second product from the product folder to show how it looks if you are not adding submodules, but rather cloning a repository that is already using submodules.

```
/product/include$ cd ..
/product$ cd ..
$ git clone product product_alpha
```

```
Cloning into 'product_alpha'...
done.
```

```
$ cd product_alpha/
/product_alpha$ ls
include   product.h
/product_alpha$ ls include/
```

In our freshly cloned repository, the include folder exists, but it is empty. The following log statement shows that we do indeed have the newest commit on the project repository. So the issue must be with the submodule itself.

```
/product_alpha$ git log
commit ebb028e42833ba80df82f1694257e646d26436d1 (HEAD -> master, origin/
master, origin/HEAD)
Author: Johan Abildskov <randomsort@gmail.com>
Date:    Tue Aug 4 20:57:06 2020 +0200

    Update include

commit f7a101df8286b36cd2abee11cd878306c5b89a7b
Author: Johan Abildskov <randomsort@gmail.com>
Date:    Tue Aug 4 20:50:24 2020 +0200

    Add component

commit 53e5bf7ed2455e9aa578ff1f9a7bdd7a09eb4c21
Author: Johan Abildskov <randomsort@gmail.com>
Date:    Tue Aug 4 20:47:44 2020 +0200

    Touch product header
```

After cloning a repository using submodules, we first need to init the submodules. Initialization is required to populate the local repository configuration correctly.

```
/product_alpha$ git submodule init
Submodule 'include' (/home/randomsort/repos/git-katas/submodules/exercise/
remote) registered for path 'include'
/product_alpha$ ls include
```

The still frustratingly empty include directory tells us that it is not enough to initialize the submodule. We use update to check out the submodule to the relevant path.

```
/product_alpha$ git submodule update
Cloning into '/home/randomsort/repos/git-katas/submodules/exercise/product_
alpha/include'...
done.
Submodule path 'include': checked out
'19451c07652a282a71eeb7d953d9d807c66284a8'
/product_alpha$ ls include
component.h  file
```

So we did not get the newest change on the submodule, as we have file rather than file.txt.

```
/product_alpha$ cd ..
$ cd product
/product$ git status
On branch master
Changes not staged for commit:
  (use "git add <file>..." to update what will be committed)
  (use "git checkout -- <file>..." to discard changes in working directory)

        modified:   include (new commits)

no changes added to commit (use "git add" and/or "git commit -a")
```

As we can see, just because we made the change to the submodule in the context of the product is no guarantee that the product reflects this change. This trap is another caveat using submodules. People that have experience with other version control systems such as ClearCase might have an intuition that we can deliver a single change atomically across multiple repositories, but that is not possible in Git. While it might not feel like it, changes in the submodule and in the products using the submodule are completely independent and cannot be done as a transaction.

So let us commit the change to the submodule version in the product repository.

```
/product$ git add .
/product$ git commit -m "update submodule"
[master 6102bac] update submodule
 1 file changed, 1 insertion(+), 1 deletion(-)
/product$ cd ..
$ cd product_alpha/
/product_alpha$ git submodule update
/product_alpha$ git pull
```

```
remote: Counting objects: 2, done.
remote: Compressing objects: 100% (2/2), done.
remote: Total 2 (delta 0), reused 0 (delta 0)
Unpacking objects: 100% (2/2), done.
From /home/randomsort/repos/git-katas/submodules/exercise/product
    ebb028e..6102bac  master      -> origin/master
Updating ebb028e..6102bac
Fast-forward
 include | 2 +-
 1 file changed, 1 insertion(+), 1 deletion(-)
/product_alpha$ ls include
component.h  file
/product_alpha$ git submodule update
Submodule path 'include': checked out
'd9ba3247bb58bfc4f36ed3d6fa60781b0b32a5e1'
/product_alpha$ ls include/
component.h  file.txt
```

Here, we again notice the two-step approach to getting a change from a submodule. First, we update the reference to the submodule, and then we make the local path reflect the content of the submodule at that reference.

This exercise walked you through working with submodules. As you can see, the tooling is quite easy to use. The difficulties with submodules come from nontrivial usage where it can become hard to keep track of what is going on.

This section has covered Git Submodules, so you now should have an idea about how they work and what you can do with them. I still recommend going with the native dependency management tooling if there is one available for the framework that you are using.

Git Large File Storage

Git is excellent at managing text files, which is the polite way of saying that Git is not very suited at storing binary files. Large binary assets, in particular, are taxing in Git. This is caused by Git's offline capabilities, where the distributed nature of Git puts all versions in each of our clones. This can cause a lot of bandwidth and storage usage, which might make Git slow to work with.

My first take when people want to store binary assets in Git is to tell them not to. In the general case, storing binary assets in Git is a workaround rather than a real solution. A proper artifact management strategy together with a binary repository manager, such as JFrog Artifactory or Sonatype Nexus, usually is the best solution. There can be scenarios where it is useful to save binary assets in Git, and if this is necessary, in my opinion, the only right way to do this is using Git LFS. The primary cost in terms of workflow of using Git LFS is that you no longer can work truly offline. Depending on connectivity and size of binary assets, this is a smaller problem today than it was five or ten years ago.

These days Git LFS is bundled with most installers. You can test if you have it installed with the command `git lfs`. If it doesn't error, you have Git LFS on your computer. If you lack Git LFS, you can download and install it from `https://git-lfs.github.com/`.

Implementation

Although invisible to daily users, I believe understanding the shape of the Git LFS implementation helps with the intuition around what parts of your workflow will have changed fundamentally from a non-Git LFS workflow. Git LFS uses some features that we covered previously, namely, filters and Git attributes.

Git LFS uses Git attributes to track which paths should be processed through LFS, rather than Git's normal persistence model. Filters are used to substitute the read and write operations of plain Git, with those from Git LFS.

In order to be able to work with Git LFS, the repository manager that you are using needs to support it. The large Git repository managers support Git LFS out of the box. Some need a secondary storage to put the large files in, while others are able to maintain them on a stand-alone basis. Consult the documentation for your specific repository manager.

What happens when you track a path with Git LFS is that it will not write the full binary object to the repository, but rather an empty dummy file. When the commit is pushed, rather than pushing directly to the repository, it will be offloaded to the secondary storage defined by the repository configuration on the central host. When you check out a tracked path, Git LFS will, if necessary, download that file from secondary storage and then check out that file to the given path. Except that you are unable to work in offline mode when switching to previously non-checked-out versions, this will function completely transparent. Figure 8-3 shows this workflow.

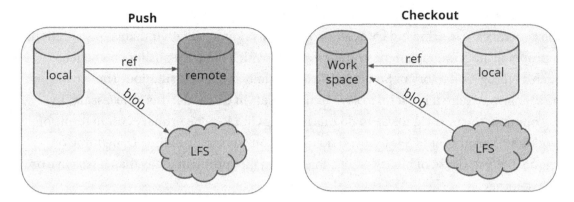

Figure 8-3. *Git LFS flow showing uploading to secondary storage during push and downloading during a checkout*

So rather than retrieving all commits with all objects when fetching, some objects are not fetched by Git until they are needed by a given checkout.

Tracking Files with Git LFS

In this section, we cover working with new files added to Git LFS. Later, we cover how to remove large assets from your repository and moving them to Git LFS. Initially, we need to run the command git lfs install to initialize Git LFS. This should only be done once per local repository. After having done that, we can add paths to track using git lfs track path. This will create an entry in the .gitattributes file, with the relevant properties. Commonly, we want to track patterns of paths rather than concrete paths. This removes the need for us to explicitly add all binary assets that we want to track with LFS individually. So we'd rather use git lfs track *.iso than git lfs track image.iso.

After running the command git lfs track *.iso, the .gitattributes file should contain the following:

```
*.iso filter=lfs diff=lfs merge=lfs -text
```

This means that whenever someone adds an ISO to our repository, it will be handled by Git LFS. Assuming that your remote supports Git LFS, this is all you need to do.

As we covered earlier, commits are immutable, so this does not clean up binary assets that were previously added to the repository. We cover how to find them and clean them up in the next sections.

Git Sizer

It is not uncommon to have a feeling that working with one of your repositories is clunky. Often, we even have a good idea about what is making the repository bothersome to work with. But, if we are going to do a huge undertaking, like cleaning up our repository, we should not do it on a gut feeling, we should do it based on a database. Fortunately, there are free tools that can help us investigate our repository. One such tool is git-sizer https://github.com/github/git-sizer. git-sizer allows us to analyze repositories and report common problems with big Git repositories. Listing 8-2 shows a snapshot from analyzing the DevOpsDays Assets repository. Even though it primarily contains binary assets, a common cause of a repository that is too big, Git sizer only reports one problematic asset. This shows that Git can be used sensibly for assets, if done right. The DevOpsDays web team has also separated binary assets from the code base to make it easier to work with.

Listing 8-2. Report from Git sizer

```
/pg-lfs$ ~/git-sizer

Processing blobs: 5
Processing trees: 4
Processing commits: 4
Matching commits to trees: 4
Processing annotated tags: 0
Processing references: 3
| Name                        | Value     | Level of concern              |
| --------------------------- | --------- | ----------------------------- |
| Biggest objects             |           |                               |
| * Blobs                     |           |                               |
|   * Maximum size       [1] |  81.6 MiB | ********                      |

[1]  6660801deb787c5d0fa941801c73dd573381c4c6 (refs/heads/master:alpine-
rpi-3.12.0-armv7.tar.gz)
```

This report can be useful to determine if there are particular aspects of the repository that we can address. The README of the git-sizer repository contains some remedies for different Git repository size ailments. In our case, we are looking for problematic binary assets, and now that we know how to use git-sizer to locate them, we move on to using the BFG repo cleaner to move those files to Git LFS.

Converting a Repository to Git LFS

Now that we can detect problematic files that are already present in our repository, we are ready to clean up the repository and make it a bit more efficient in our workflow.

We can use the BFG repo cleaner to remove unwanted files from our history. This unwanted data can be sensitive information that we would prefer not have in the history or more commonly binary assets that we either never should have added, or that have grown problematic over time.

Caution   We are now moving into potentially dangerous territory. As long as we are careful, these operations should be safe, but there are potentially destructive, nonrecoverable scenarios that can occur. If, however, we are deliberate and move with caution, we can prefer any unexpected incidents.

We can use Git LFS to rewrite our history and add problematic paths to Git LFS.

CONVERT TO LFS

This exercise involves forking a repository from GitHub and working in that, so complete it in your terminal, wherever you put your repositories. Start by heading to `https://github.com/randomsort/practical-git-lfs` and create a fork of that repository to your account. In this exercise, I work from the fork `pg-lfs`. Note that this exercise requires a remote that supports Git LFS. GitHub does this, but you might need to enable it on your settings page.

First off, I clone the repository that I work in, in this exercise. Replace the URL with your personal fork.

```
$ git clone git@github.com:randomsort/pg-lfs
Cloning into 'pg-lfs'...
remote: Enumerating objects: 13, done.
remote: Total 13 (delta 0), reused 0 (delta 0), pack-reused 13
Receiving objects: 100% (13/13), 81.64 MiB | 11.28 MiB/s, done.
Resolving deltas: 100% (2/2), done.
```

It is not apparent from the printed terminal output, but this took a long, tedious time, which we know kills developer productivity and motivation. So we look to see if we can find a problem.

```
$ cd pg-lfs
/pg-lfs$ ls
LICENSE  README.md  alpine-rpi-3.12.0-armv7.tar.gz
```

We note that there is a tar.gz file and that the Git folder is large compared to such a small repository. We run `git-sizer` to find out if there are any problems.

```
/pg-lfs$ du -s -h .git
82M     .git
/pg-lfs$ ~/git-sizer

Processing blobs: 5
Processing trees: 4
Processing commits: 4
Matching commits to trees: 4
Processing annotated tags: 0
Processing references: 3
| Name                        | Value    | Level of concern               |
| --------------------------- | -------- | ------------------------------ |
| Biggest objects             |          |                                |
| * Blobs                     |          |                                |
|   * Maximum size       [1] | 81.6 MiB | ********                        |
```

[1]   6660801deb787c5d0fa941801c73dd573381c4c6 (refs/heads/master:alpine-rpi-3.12.0-armv7.tar.gz)

From the output of `git-sizer`, we see that at least a `tar.gz` file is problematic. We decide it would be good to store `tar.gz` files in Git LFS, rather than directly in the Git repository. We can use the `git lfs migrate` tool for that. We pass the patterns and references we want Git LFS to treat.

```
/pg-lfs$ git lfs migrate import --include="*.tar.gz" --include-ref=master
migrate: Sorting commits: ..., done
migrate: Rewriting commits: 100% (4/4), done
  master         9a3d24f44a28e5f514633b834afbe6022062febe ->
873439a4869e29b388027465e2a488d68c977df2
migrate: Updating refs: ..., done
migrate: checkout: ..., done
/pg-lfs$ git status
On branch master
Your branch and 'origin/master' have diverged,
```

and have 4 and 4 different commits each, respectively.
  (use "git pull" to merge the remote branch into yours)

nothing to commit, working tree clean

Git status tells us that we have all different commits and that our working directory is clean. In this scenario, this shows that we have no commits in common with our remote.

```
/pg-lfs$ ls -al
total 4
drwxrwxrwx 1 randomsort randomsort  512 Aug  4 22:06 .
drwxrwxrwx 1 randomsort randomsort  512 Aug  4 22:03 ..
drwxrwxrwx 1 randomsort randomsort  512 Aug  4 22:06 .git
-rw-rw-rw- 1 randomsort randomsort   45 Aug  4 22:06 .gitattributes
-rw-rw-rw- 1 randomsort randomsort 1080 Aug  4 22:03 LICENSE
-rw-rw-rw- 1 randomsort randomsort  287 Aug  4 22:03 README.md
-rw-rw-rw- 1 randomsort randomsort  133 Aug  4 22:06 alpine-rpi-3.12.0-armv7.tar.gz
randomsort@DESKTOP-3196DO6:~/repos/lfs2$ cat .gitattributes
*.tar.gz filter=lfs diff=lfs merge=lfs -text
```

The Git LFS migration added the correct entry to .gitattributes, retroactively. We are happy with the state of our repository and push to the remote.

```
/pg-lfs$ git push --force
Counting objects: 14, done.
Delta compression using up to 4 threads.
Compressing objects: 100% (8/8), done.
Writing objects: 100% (14/14), 2.34 KiB | 2.34 MiB/s, done.
Total 14 (delta 3), reused 14 (delta 3)
remote: Resolving deltas: 100% (3/3), done.
remote: This repository moved. Please use the new location:
remote:    git@github.com:RandomSort/pg-lfs.git
To github.com:randomsort/pg-lfs
 + 9a3d24f...873439a master -> master (forced update)
```

A force push should not be done leisurely, and as mentioned earlier, we should use --force-with-lease, but that does not work in this case as we have no common history. After pushing to the remote, we clone to a separate location to see if we saved any space.

```
/pg-lfs$ cd ..
$ git clone git@github.com:randomsort/pg-lfs lfs2
```

```
Cloning into 'lfs2'...
remote: Enumerating objects: 10, done.
remote: Counting objects: 100% (10/10), done.
remote: Compressing objects: 100% (6/6), done.
remote: Total 14 (delta 3), reused 10 (delta 3), pack-reused 4
Receiving objects: 100% (14/14), done.
Resolving deltas: 100% (3/3), done.
$ cd lfs2
/lfs2$ du -s -h .git
48K     .git
/lfs2$ ls
LICENSE  README.md  alpine-rpi-3.12.0-armv7.tar.gz
```

Even though our workspace looks the same, our Git repository is only a fraction of the size. 48K compared to 82M is a difference that we cannot fathom without experiencing it. This will have an impact on developer quality of life and have an impact on automation.

Remember to delete your fork so you don't take up unnecessary resources at GitHub :).

This exercise showed how easy it is to slice a part of your repository out if it hurts you in terms of size.

Git Katas

To support the learning goals of this chapter, complete the following katas:

- Bisect
- Submodules

Summary

In this chapter, we learned how to manage dependencies using submodules, to find bad changesets efficiently using Git bisect, and finally to remove problematic assets from our repositories with Git LFS.

I sincerely hope that none of these will be useful for you on a day-to-day basis, as they represent corner cases. But now you are aware should the need arise for one of these specialized Git features.

CHAPTER 9

Git Internals

As the book comes closer to its end, I will use a few pages geeking out about some of the internals of Git, to help solidify the mental models and demystify the bowels of Git. The purpose of this chapter is not to be thorough or exhaustive, nor will it allow you to become a contributor to Git, though I do encourage everyone to consider contributing to open source. We will open up the hood of Git and see how some of the components are wired together, such that we can better reason about what is going on, and should the worst come to worst, we can dig deep.

The Git Graph

At the base level, Git is a graph of commits with labels. This graph is a so-called directed acyclic graph, which has some interesting properties. Graph Theory is a mature and widely studied area of computer science. Many of the foundational algorithms of Git are from the domain of Graph Theory.

© Johan Abildskov 2020
J. Abildskov, *Practical Git*, https://doi.org/10.1007/978-1-4842-6270-2_9

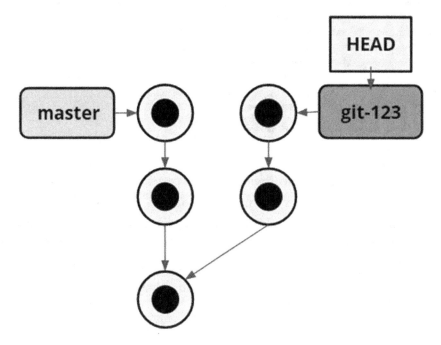

Figure 9-1. *A Git graph of commits with parent pointers between them. Two branches and HEAD are added*

A graph is defined as a set of vertices and edges between them. In Git, a vertex is implemented as a commit, with edges being represented as the parent pointers on a commit. Figure 9-1 shows a Git graph with edges and vertices. That the graph is directed means that each edge has a direction and thus can be considered an arrow. Acyclic means that there are no cycles in the graph of commits. It is therefore not possible to return to a commit by following the parent pointers outbound. This has consequences for the validity of the algorithms Git uses. We are not going to go into any depth with the graph theoretic background, but where relevant I will introduce the term in this chapter.

Commits

In the previous chapters, we have considered commits as the basic atomic unit, the most fundamental part of Git. But much as an atom can be decomposed into neutrons, protons, and electrons, we can break a commit apart into its composite elements. As we have been versioning workspaces and discussing how these versions relate to another, the commit is an appropriate level of abstraction. Commits are also the level of abstraction that we work with in normal Git operations during software development.

A commit is composed of metadata such as ID, author, message, timestamp, and parent pointer(s). The commit also contains a pointer to a tree, which is the data structure that Git uses to store the state of the working directory. The commit data structure is shown in Figure 9-2.

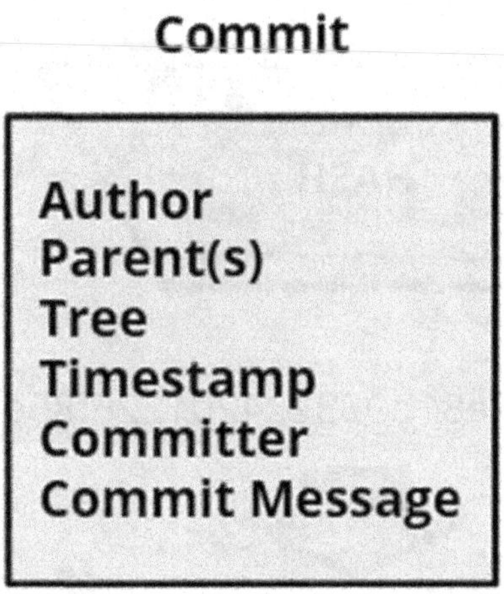

Commit

Figure 9-2. *The data contained in a commit*

A crucial part of the commit data structure is the ID, the unique identifier for a given commit. Git generates these unique IDs deterministically based on the content of the commit. Git does this through a hash function. Hash functions have the property that if their input changes, it is unpredictable what the output will become. We can safely assume that if two commits have the same ID, they have the same content and are thus the same commit. Git stores objects in .git/objects/ in a folder named the first two characters of the ID, in a file named the 38 last characters of the ID. The commit c70be832f3c02582ed3b587b282aa1c034f5dc1b thus lives in the folder .git/objects/c7/ in the file 0be832f3c02582ed3b587b282aa1c034f5dc1b for a full path of .git/objects/c7/ 0be832f3c02582ed3b587b282aa1c034f5dc1b.

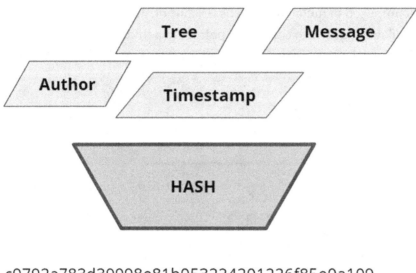

c9792a783d39998e81b953224201226f85e0a109

.git/objects/c9/792a783d39998e81b953224201226f85e0a109

Figure 9-3. *Hashing content to a file system address*

The preceding property is the reason Git is sometimes referred to as being content-addressable. The content defines the ID and thus the address at which the content is stored. As we cover in the next section, the tree also has an ID determined by its content, which means that the ID of a commit is uniquely determined by its directory content and metadata. Note that there can exist multiple commits with the same directory contents but different metadata, even within a single repository.

A commit contains all this information. We can investigate the commit at HEAD using the command show. We can pass it a ref, and without any, it will default to HEAD. Show also appends the diff, demonstrating the changeset in Listing 9-1.

Listing 9-1. Using git show to display information about a commit

```
$ git log -1
commit 1135048cd36443eee6e28b472aa203b61997087b (HEAD -> master, origin/
master, origin/HEAD)
Author: Johan Abildskov <randomsort@gmail.com>
Date:    Thu May 21 13:35:18 2020 +0200

    Add the Practical Git Bio

$ git show
commit 1135048cd36443eee6e28b472aa203b61997087b (HEAD -> master, origin/
master, origin/HEAD)
Author: Johan Abildskov <randomsort@gmail.com>
Date:    Thu May 21 13:35:18 2020 +0200

    Add the Practical Git Bio

diff --git a/the-practical-git.md b/the-practical-git.md
new file mode 100644
index 0000000..7e8aac9
--- /dev/null
+++ b/the-practical-git.md
@@ -0,0 +1,11 @@
+# The Practical Git
+
+Hi,
+I am the first to submit a pull request to this repository and I am so
happy to do it!
+
+I represent the book, so I am a part of an exercise, how exciting is this?!?
+
+Other than that, I hope you enjoy the book and contribute your bio to this
repository!
+
+Cheers,
+The Practical Git
```

The output contains valuable information, but some of the information, like the diff, is calculated. In scenarios where we want to investigate the raw content, we use the command `git cat-file`. Cat-file allows us to output Git objects directly and if we use the flag `-p` in a human-readable, rather than binary, format. I have only ever run into two ways of using `cat-file`: using `-p` to investigate the content and using `-s` to check the size. In Listing 9-2, I show running `cat-file -p` and `-s` to see the size of the commit and the content as stored on disk. Digging deep like this is useful when hooks and filters might interfere with a naïve workspace investigation.

Listing 9-2. Using cat-file -p and -s to investigate a commit

```
$ git cat-file -p 11350
tree e119db480900fac506e721d6560fce9ffcc0765f
parent ce866b9f738529476f87347a76b0ba69e5ff0960
author Johan Abildskov <randomsort@gmail.com> 1590060918 +0200
committer Johan Abildskov <randomsort@gmail.com> 1590060918 +0200

Add the Practical Git Bio

$ git cat-file -s 113504
250
```

In Listing 9-2, we see the tree reference that we mentioned earlier. This tree object contains the data on the root of the working directory that we are versioning. The data contained in Listing 9-2 uniquely determines the commit ID, and directory content uniquely determines the tree ID.

Trees

While we at the abstract level have a Git graph of commits with pointers between them, at the more concrete level, we are interested in the evolution of working directories and how they relate. The tree object is what keeps track of a directory on a file system.

Trees contain lists of paths along with a type and reference to the object that needs to be restored to that path. As trees can also reference trees, this allows Git to restore a full working directory with nested folders. A path can reference either a tree, blob, or commit. Trees represent nested folders, blobs file content, and commits submodules to be instantiated at that path. An example tree listing is shown in Listing 9-3.

Listing 9-3. A tree listing

```
$ git cat-file -p 4f66
100644 blob f5b7a1a105b79d9b0bd889c4ba9c3feba88687fc        README.md
100644 blob 9b2c04de2d845c775fa98f86fcf2bed7f0bf1549        setup.ps1
100755 blob 20cbad89573a7f1472e9bd2bcafd8441eedfecef        setup.sh
040000 tree 85d92a502a5fa0297480932721ccd07c91bb9ef6        utils
```

In the next section, we will show how blobs work which will allow us to draw the full image of Git's internal data representation. An interesting point to make here is that the blob solely contains the content of the file to be restored at that given path. This means that the names in the tree listing are solely responsible for what a given file will be called in the directory structure. This is also how Git does deduplication of files. Since the same content will end up with the same hashed ID, multiple copies of the same file will not take up space in the repository. Trees also reside in `.git/objects`.

Blobs

Blobs are file content storage. Our intuition tells us that a file consists of a path including the name, and some content. In Git, it is the tree or the folder abstraction that handles path and filename information, so the only responsibility left for the blob is managing the file content. IDs in Git are generated through hashing content using the sha1 or sha256 algorithms. As mentioned previously, Git is considered content-addressable. That is perhaps most evident when discussion blobs as their address, or file path, are directly calculated from file content. The following code shows how changing a file a little changes the blob ID unpredictably:

```
$ ls -alh
total 24K
drwxr-xr-x 1 rando 197609     0 aug 10 14:30 ./
drwxr-xr-x 1 rando 197609     0 aug 10 14:29 ../
drwxr-xr-x 1 rando 197609     0 aug 10 14:31 .git/
-rw-r--r-- 1 rando 197609 8,1K aug 10 14:31 file.txt
```

```
$ git cat-file -p HEAD
tree b8041d12e65e591d4921bc3edfc9cabc23f9565a
author Johan Abildskov <randomsort@gmail.com> 1597062696 +0200
committer Johan Abildskov <randomsort@gmail.com> 1597062696 +0200

First commit

$ git cat-file -p b8041d12e65e591d4921bc3edfc9cabc23f9565a
100644 blob 02454bc2cea1cdbce18a1cdcc39d94fad5a9777f    file.txt

$ echo " " >> file.txt

$ git add .

$ git commit -m "update file"
[master da9a6db] update file
 1 file changed, 1 insertion(+), 1 deletion(-)

$ git cat-file -p HEAD
tree 243983d2cef9f535fd2a6d728958e0b09398bf72
parent 41e1a39ebc9c3720d60945c95bd4bd7152dbc907
author Johan Abildskov <randomsort@gmail.com> 1597062777 +0200
committer Johan Abildskov <randomsort@gmail.com> 1597062777 +0200

update file

$ git cat-file -p 243983d2cef9f535fd2a6d728958e0b09398bf72
100644 blob 2f7720fb6a49470af72fbc2b56061e1871320c93    file.txt
```

In the preceding code, appending a whitespace character changes the ID from 02454bc2cea1cdbce18a1cdcc39d94fad5a9777f to 243983d2cef9f535fd2a6d728958e0b09398bf72, two strings that have no obvious connection. This is a property of hash functions. Another property of the hash function is that collisions are so unlikely that they in practice do not happen. Collisions are when two different inputs generate the same output. A reason for Git to migrate from sha1 to sha256 is keeping collision generation difficult in the face of modern computing power. The consequence of this is that it is impossible to have duplicate file contents, even with different file names. It is also practically impossible to overwrite a file with content that are different, as that would require a collision.

References

In Git, we have three reference types: branches, tags, and remotes. References are lightweight with the exception of annotated tags. Lightweight means there is no additional information attached to it, but it is a simple pointer.

Branches live in `.git/refs/heads`, while tags reside in .git/refs/tags. Remotes are present in `.git/refs/remotes` and from our perspective can be seen as read-only branches. This is because updating them should always come from an operation involving fetching the information from the remote, rather than manipulating them locally. As we discussed when covering branches earlier, references break our intuition and mental model of how branches look and behave. In Git, references are labels that mark a specific commit, such that it is easier to retrieve than by the ID directly. Tags can be considered branches that are not moving.

HEAD is a special pointer that refers to what is currently checked out. HEAD can either point to a local branch or a commit. If we try to switch to either a remote branch or a tag, we will end up in detached HEAD state. In this case, we can lose our work because new commits will not by default have a reference to them, so after some time, they will be garbage collected.

The detached HEAD scenario is shown in the following code listing:

```
$ git log --oneline --decorate
da9a6db (HEAD -> master, tag: test) update file
41e1a39 First commit

$ git switch test
fatal: a branch is expected, got tag 'test'

$ git checkout test
Note: switching to 'test'.
```

You are in 'detached HEAD' state. You can look around, make experimental changes and commit them, and you can discard any commits you make in this state without impacting any branches by switching back to a branch.

If you want to create a new branch to retain commits you create, you may do so (now or later) by using -c with the switch command. Example:

```
  git switch -c <new-branch-name>
```

Or undo this operation with:

```
  git switch -
```

Turn off this advice by setting config variable advice.detachedHead to false

HEAD is now at da9a6db update file

The solution here is to either create a new pointer to work from or check out an already existing pointer to the relevant commit.

While our branches are not containing any information per se, the metainformation they contain can be important for traceability – and asking such questions as where was the master branch before I did this hard reset. For that, we can use git reflog. If we pass a reference to git reflog, we get a list of how that pointer changed. We can then use the references in there to check out commits based on where a reference has been. Most commonly, we use indexes such as master@{1}, meaning where the master reference was one change ago. There are also more abstract references such as master@{yesterday} or master@{upstream} to check out where the tracking branch for master points at. The following screenshot shows using the reflog in a trivial linear example. Where it becomes really interesting is more complex history.

Listing 9-4. Using `git reflog` to investigate where a pointer has been

```
$ git reflog
da9a6db (HEAD -> master, tag: test) HEAD@{0}: checkout: moving from
41e1a39ebc9c3720d60945c95bd4bd7152dbc907 to master
41e1a39 HEAD@{1}: checkout: moving from master to master@{1}
da9a6db (HEAD -> master, tag: test) HEAD@{2}: checkout: moving from
da9a6dbe39f09e98520f208e2b94ec610af1af4f to master
da9a6db (HEAD -> master, tag: test) HEAD@{3}: checkout: moving from master
to test
da9a6db (HEAD -> master, tag: test) HEAD@{4}: commit: update file
41e1a39 HEAD@{5}: commit (initial): First commit

$ git checkout master@{1}
Note: switching to 'master@{1}'.
```

You are in 'detached HEAD' state. You can look around, make experimental changes and commit them, and you can discard any commits you make in this state without impacting any branches by switching back to a branch.

If you want to create a new branch to retain commits you create, you may do so (now or later) by using -c with the switch command. Example:

```
git switch -c <new-branch-name>
```

Or undo this operation with:

```
git switch -
```

Turn off this advice by setting config variable advice.detachedHead to false

HEAD is now at 41e1a39 First commit

Note that the reflog is a purely local concept and is not shared across multiple clones of the same repository.

Versioning with Trees

We have covered all the constituent parts, so we have the framework to discuss how versioning works in Git. We have HEAD that points to a branch, that points to a commit, that points to a tree, and that tree points to blobs and trees. While the previous sentence is all we need to know, it is also shown in Figure 9-4, in an actually digestible format.

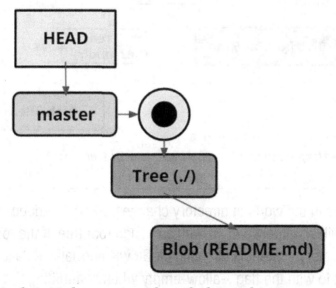

Figure 9-4. *A single initial commit with underlying objects*

In Figure 9-4, a single commit with corresponding Git object structure is shown. This looks remarkable as a one-to-one mapping of a file system. And the really interesting part happens when we add more commits. Git will reuse as much as possible from already existing commits. This comes for free given the content-addressable nature of Git. This means that only the trees that contain changes will need to be created, as the trees that already exist will be reused as they have the correct address. During a commit operation, no blob objects will be removed; it is rather an additive procedure only creating the blobs needed to represent the current working directory. This reuse is why Git isn't greedily globbing up your hard drive with all the different versions you have around. Figure 9-5 shows how changing a file creates new tree and blob objects while reusing the unchanged ones.

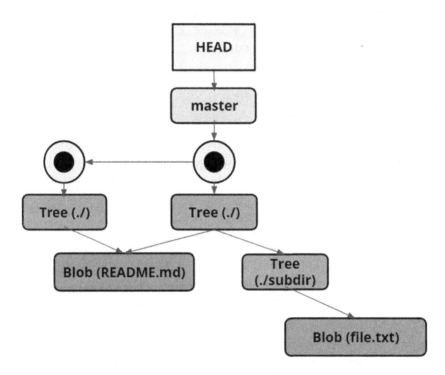

Figure 9-5. *Creating a commit reuses objects and tree*

Note   If any file in the working directory changes, by being added, deleted, or modified, this will ultimately end up with a change root tree. If the room tree is unchanged, directory content is unchanged. Git will normally not accept this, but you can force it to with the flag --allow-empty when committing.

GIT INTERNALS

In this exercise, we start with an empty repository and slowly investigate what parts are showing up in our repository as we add content. This exercise starts by creating an empty repository locally, so you can start where you have a command line. Note that all IDs will be different from what you see in the exercise, so if you naively copy paste the commands, they are unlikely to succeed.

We start by initializing an empty repository and poke around to see what we can find.

```
$ git init pg-internals
Initialized empty Git repository in /user/randomsort/pg-internals/.git/
$ cd pg-internals/
$ ls -al .git
total 24
drwxr-xr-x. 4 randomsort users 4096 Aug 11 13:43 .
drwxr-xr-x. 3 randomsort users 4096 Aug 11 13:43 ..
-rw-r--r--. 1 randomsort users   92 Aug 11 13:43 config
-rw-r--r--. 1 randomsort users   23 Aug 11 13:43 HEAD
drwxr-xr-x. 4 randomsort users 4096 Aug 11 13:43 objects
drwxr-xr-x. 4 randomsort users 4096 Aug 11 13:43 refs
$ ls .git/objects
info  pack
```

The first interesting part to note is that the object folder is empty except for the info and pack folders. These are folders used for Git's compression. They are empty in a newly initialized repository.

```
$ ls .git/refs
heads  tags
$ ls .git/refs/heads
```

We have the refs folders, but we can see there are no branches.

```
$ cat .git/HEAD
ref: refs/heads/master
```

HEAD is still pointing to the master branch even though it does not exist. This is a situation where a corner case just needs to be handled. Either HEAD would not exist, the branch it points to not exist, or the object the branch points to be missing. From the following status command, we can see that Git is clearly aware of the situation, but if we try to check out the master branch, we get an error.

175

```
$ git status
On branch master

No commits yet

nothing to commit (create/copy files and use "git add" to track)
$ git checkout master
error: pathspec 'master' did not match any file(s) known to git
```

Let's create the first commit.

```
$ echo "# First data" > README.md
$ git add README.md
$ git commit -m "Initial Commit"
[master (root-commit) 2fb5c2e] Initial Commit
 1 file changed, 1 insertion(+)
 create mode 100644 README.md
```

After having created the first commit, we expect to see three objects in the `.git/objects` folders: one for the commit, one for the tree, and one for the blob.

```
$ ls .git/objects
2f  bf  d4  info  pack
$ ls .git/objects/2f
b5c2e86d6f21d52d2f05b07ed524669f10d07f
```

Without being thorough, we can see we have three objects. We can use cat-file to check the content of any given object here. We note that the ID of the object is the folder name (`2f`) concatenated with the file name (`b5c2e86d6f21d52d2f05b07ed524669f10d07f`). Similar to when we reference commits, we can use a unique prefix of the full ID.

```
$ git cat-file -p 2fb5c
tree bfd4eb4e8767678f4abfe229f7ee701ca9ee0b69
author Johan Abildskov <randomsort@gmail.com> 1597146899 +0200
committer Johan Abildskov <randomsort@gmail.com> 1597146899 +0200

Initial Commit
```

So it seems we hit the commit object in this scenario.

Now we create a subdirectory with a file to see how that changes our objects.

```
$ mkdir subdir
$ echo "important content" > subdir/file.txt
$ git add subdir/file.txt
$ git commit -m "Add important content"
[master 62b545d] Add important content
 1 file changed, 1 insertion(+)
 create mode 100644 subdir/file.txt
$ ls .git/objects
24  2f  3a  62  bf  c9  d4  info  pack
```

Here, we see we end up with seven objects compared to the three in the initial commit. We end up with this because we create a new commit, a new root tree object, a tree object for subdir, and a blob object for the file – plus, the original three objects that are still around. We are not creating a new blob for README.md as it is unchanged and will be reused. We can use cat-file again to see the content of the new commit, and note that we have a new tree object.

```
$ git cat-file -p HEAD
tree 3a7a21c251d2e8c05a6c1c7c2c866c4c3821e97e
parent 2fb5c2e86d6f21d52d2f05b07ed524669f10d07f
author Johan Abildskov <randomsort@gmail.com> 1597147088 +0200
committer Johan Abildskov <randomsort@gmail.com> 1597147088 +0200

Add important content
```

Git filters and drivers can cause Git repository content to be different in the working directory than in the repository. This is true in the case of Git LFS, but it could also be local configuration such as line endings.

In the case where we want to see what is really stored in Git, we can use `git ls-tree` to find what the blob is for a given path at a given point in time. In the following line, we tell Git to go through trees recursively and search for subdir/file.txt in the revision HEAD. Instead of HEAD, we could have provided an arbitrary tree or commit object.

```
$ git ls-tree -r HEAD subdir/file.txt
100644 blob 24013f7d4de4b5143b03c76db8656625c00798d2    subdir/file.txt
```

Now that we have tinkered with objects, let's manipulate a few branches. First, let's see what branches are present.

```
$ git branch
* master
$ ls .git/refs/heads
master
```

We have the master branch, and we can see it is now also present in refs/ heads. We can conclude that the file representing the branch was created when we made the first commit.

Under normal circumstances we use Git to create branches, but it is trivial to do so manually.

```
$ cp .git/refs/heads/master .git/refs/heads/practical-git
$ git branch
* master
  practical-git
```

By the magic of a copy command, we have created a new branch. The consequence of this is that creating a branch is tremendously cheap, as all the file contains is the sha of the commit. HEAD points to master, so let's check out our other branch.

```
$ echo "ref: refs/heads/practical-git" > .git/HEAD
$ git status
On branch practical-git
nothing to commit, working tree clean
```

As we can see, we successfully switched branches, manually. There is of course the caveat that our status would potentially be tremendously different if the branches are not pointing to the same commit.

Katas

To support the learning goal of this chapter, I recommend you to go through the following katas:

- Investigation

- Reset (You did this exercise earlier, but now you should have a better foundation to reason about what is going on. Remember to use reflog!)

Summary

This chapter has walked you through some of Git's internal structures to further build your understanding how Git is working. Except for the reflog, you should never have to dig this deep again, but I hope that you enjoyed the trip!

Index

© Johan Abildskov 2020
J. Abildskov, *Practical Git*, https://doi.org/10.1007/978-1-4842-6270-2

Printed in the United States
By Bookmasters